Empanada Recipes

Discover a Classic Latin Savory Pie with Easy Empanada Recipes in a Delicious Empanada Cookbook

By
BookSumo Press

Published by
http://www.booksumo.com

Table of Contents

Empanadas
Madeira

🥄 Prep Time: 15 mins

🕐 Total Time: 35 mins

Servings per Recipe: 8	
Calories	303.5 kcal
Fat	23.4 g
Cholesterol	162.9 mg
Sodium	529.2 mg
Carbohydrates	12.5 g
Protein	10.6 g

Ingredients

6 oz. cream cheese, softened
1 tsp. dried parsley
3/4 tsp. seasoning salt
1/4 tsp. pepper
2/3 C. sharp cheddar cheese, shredded
2 tbsp. butter
5 eggs, beaten

1 (7 1/3 oz.) cans refrigerated jumbo flaky biscuits
8 slices bacon, cooked and crumbled
1 egg white, slightly beaten
1-2 tsp. sesame seeds

Directions

1. Set your oven to 375 degrees F before doing anything else and grease a 15x10-inch jelly roll pan.
2. In a bowl, add the cheese, parsley, seasoning salt and pepper and mix until well combined.
3. Add the cheese and stir to combine.
4. In a skillet, add the butter over medium heat and cook until melted.
5. Add the eggs and cook until eggs begin to set on the bottom, without stirring.
6. Now, with a spatula, stir the eggs to form large curds.
7. Cook until eggs become slightly thick, stirring continuously.
8. Remove from the heat and keep aside to cool.
9. With your hands, flatten each biscuit into a 5-inch circle.
10. Place the cream cheese mixture over each dough circle, leaving about 1/2-inch border, followed by eggs and bacon.
11. Fold the dough over the filling and press the edges to seal.
12. In the bottom of the prepared pan, arrange the empanadas about 2-inch apart.
13. Coat the top of each empanada with egg white and with the tines of a fork, press the

sealed edges.

14. Sprinkle each empanada with the sesame seeds.

15. Cook in the oven for about 14–16 minutes.

16. Remove from the oven and place the empanadas onto a wire rack to cool slightly.

17. Enjoy warm.

Buttermilk
Beef Empanadas

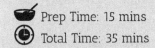 Prep Time: 15 mins

Total Time: 35 mins

Servings per Recipe: 8

Calories	303.5 kcal
Fat	23.4 g
Cholesterol	162.9 mg
Sodium	529.2 mg
Carbohydrates	12.5 g
Protein	10.6 g

Ingredients

1 tbsp. olive oil
1/2 lb. lean ground beef
1/2 green bell pepper, chopped
2 tbsp. chopped garlic
1/3 C. raisins, chopped
1/4 C. pimento stuffed olives, chopped
1 1/2 tbsp. balsamic vinegar
1 tbsp. flour

1 3/4 tsp. allspice
1 tsp. cumin
1/4 tsp. cayenne pepper
1 C. Monterey Jack cheese, grated
1/3 C. cilantro, chopped
2 (12 oz.) packages refrigerated buttermilk biscuits
1 egg, beaten with 1 tbsp. water

Directions

1. Set your oven to 375 degrees F before doing anything else and grease a baking sheet.
2. In a heavy-bottomed skillet, add the oil over medium heat and cook until heated through.
3. Add the beef, garlic and bell pepper and cook for about 6 minutes.
4. Stir in the olives, raisins, vinegar, flour, allspice, cumin and cayenne pepper and cook for about 5 minutes, mixing occasionally.
5. Stir in the salt and pepper and remove from the heat.
6. Add the cheese and cilantro and stir to combine.
7. Place the biscuits onto a lightly floured surface and roll into a 4-inch circle.
8. Coat half of each biscuit with the egg wash.
9. Place about 1 rounded tbsp.. filling onto each dough circle.
10. Fold the dough over the filling and press the edges to seal.
11. In the bottom of the prepared baking sheet, arrange the empanadas and coat each with the egg wash.
12. Cook in the oven for about 12 minutes.
13. Enjoy warm.sealed edges.

14. Sprinkle each empanada with the sesame seeds.
15. Cook in the oven for about 14-16 minutes.
16. Remove from the oven and place the empanadas onto a wire rack to cool slightly.
17. Enjoy warm.

Empanadas
in Calabasas

Prep Time: 25 mins
Total Time: 38 mins

Servings per Recipe: 1
Calories	327.0 kcal
Fat	21.2 g
Cholesterol	75.9 mg
Sodium	2373.8 mg
Carbohydrates	26.8 g
Protein	8.4 g

Ingredients

1 C. cooked chicken
1/2 C. Monterey Jack cheese, grated
1/2 C. cheddar cheese, grated
1 can green chili, chopped
1 tsp. minced garlic
3 tbsp. minced green onions
1/2 tsp. cumin, ground

1 tsp. salt
2 frozen pie crusts
3 egg yolks
2 tbsp. kosher salt
1 tbsp. chili powder

Directions

1. Set your oven to 400 degrees F before doing anything else and grease a baking sheet.
2. In a bowl, add the chicken, Monterey Jack cheese, cheddar cheese, green chilies, garlic, green onions, cumin and 1 tsp. of the salt and mix until well combined.
3. Place in the fridge until using.
4. Place the pie crusts onto a floured surface and roll each one.
5. Now, cut 4-inch circles from each pie crust.
6. Place about 2 tbsp. of the chicken mixture onto the center of each dough circle.
7. Fold the dough over the filling and press the edges to seal.
8. In the bottom of the prepared baking sheet, arrange the empanadas.
9. Coat the top of each empanada with the egg yolks and dust with the kosher salt and chili powder.
10. Cook in the oven for about 12-13 minutes.
11. Enjoy warm

TROPICAL
Empanadas

Prep Time: 30 mins
Total Time: 48 mins

Servings per Recipe: 24
Calories	203.9 kcal
Fat	8.4 g
Cholesterol	1.3 mg
Sodium	69.0 mg
Carbohydrates	30.9 g
Protein	2.0 g

Ingredients

Dough
2 1/2 C. all-purpose flour
1/2 tsp. salt
3/4 C. solid shortening
1 tbsp. sour cream
1/2 C. chilled water, plus
1 tsp. chilled water
Filling

2 (20 oz.) cans crushed pineapple, well drained
1 C. sugar
1 1/2 C. flaked coconut
1 tsp. vanilla
3 tbsp. all-purpose flour
Glaze
1/4 C. sweetened condensed milk

Directions

1. For the dough: in a bowl, sift together the flour and salt.
2. Add the shortening and with an electric mixer, beat on medium speed until a coarse meal like mixture forms.
3. Add the sour cream and stir to combine well.
4. Slowly add the water and stir until a dough ball forms.
5. Make 24 small equal sized balls from the dough and arrange onto a platter.
6. With a plastic wrap, cover the plate and place in the fridge for about 15 minutes.
7. Set your oven to 425 degrees F and grease 2 baking sheets.
8. For the filling: in a bowl, add the pineapple, coconut, sugar and vanilla and mix well.
9. Dust a smooth surface with 3 tbsp. of the flour.
10. Place each dough ball onto the floured surface and roll each into a 6-inch circle.
11. Place about 2 tbsp. of the filling onto the center of each dough circle.
12. Fold the dough over the filling and press the edges to seal.
13. In the bottom of the prepared baking sheet, arrange the empanadas and coat the top of

each with sweetened condensed milk.

14. Cook in the oven for about 18 minutes.
15. Enjoy warm..

EMPANADAS
Mayagüez

Prep Time: 20 mins
Total Time: 40 mins

Servings per Recipe: 16
Calories	231.0 kcal
Fat	10.2 g
Cholesterol	0.0 mg
Sodium	188.5 mg
Carbohydrates	31.2 g
Protein	4.8 g

Ingredients

Filling
1 (15 oz.) cans pumpkin
1/2 C. sugar
1/4 tsp. salt
1/2 tsp. cinnamon
1/4 tsp. ginger
1/8 tsp. ground cloves
Dough

1 C. water
1/4 C. sugar
1 tsp. salt
2 (1/2 oz.) package dry yeast
1/8 tsp. baking powder
1/2 tsp. cinnamon
3 C. flour, divided in half
3/4 C. vegetable shortening

Directions

1. Set your oven to 350 degrees F before doing anything else and grease a baking sheet.
2. For the filling: in a bowl, add all the ingredients and mix until well combined.
3. For the dough: in a bowl, add the sugar, yeast, baking powder, cinnamon, salt and water and with an electric mixer, beat until combined.
4. Slowly, add half of the flour, beating continuously until well combined.
5. Add the shortening and mix until well combined.
6. Slowly, add the remaining flour, beating continuously until well combined.
7. Make 4 equal sized balls from the dough and with floured hands, flatten each slightly.
8. Place each dough piece onto a lightly floured surface and roll each into 4-inch circle with 1/8-inch thickness.
9. Place about 1 1/2 tbsp. of the filling onto the center of each circle.
10. Fold the dough over the filling and press the edges to seal.
11. In the bottom of the prepared baking sheet, arrange the empanadas.
12. Cook in the oven for about 18-20 minutes.
13. Enjoy warm.

Chocolate
Hazelnut Empanadas

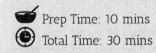 Prep Time: 10 mins

Total Time: 30 mins

Servings per Recipe: 16

Calories	232.3 kcal
Fat	13.3 g
Cholesterol	0.0 mg
Sodium	129.6 mg
Carbohydrates	25.7 g
Protein	2.5 g

Ingredients

1 large ripe banana, peeled and 1/4-inch cubes
1 C. nutella chocolate hazelnut spread
2 refrigerated 9-inch pie shells
2 tbsp. water
2 tbsp. granulated sugar
cinnamon ice cream

Directions

1. In a bowl, add the Nutella and banana and mix until well combined.
2. Place the dough onto a lightly floured surface and cut into 2 equal sized pieces.
3. Now, roll each piece into a 14x8-inch rectangle with 1/4-inch thickness.
4. With a 3-inch cookie cutter, cut 8 circles from each dough rectangle.
5. Place about 1 heaping tsp. of the Nutella mixture onto each dough circle.
6. With wet fingers, moisten the edges of each circle.
7. Fold the dough over the filling and press the edges to seal.
8. In the bottom of a foil lined baking sheet, arrange the empanadas.
9. Coat each empanada with the water and dust with the sugar.
10. Place in the freezer for about 20 minutes.
11. Set your oven to 400 degrees F.
12. Cook in the oven for about 20 minutes.
13. Enjoy warm alongside the cinnamon ice cream.

EMPANADAS
Cascada

Prep Time: 30 mins
Total Time: 40 mins

Servings per Recipe: 12
Calories	402.9 kcal
Fat	28.9 g
Cholesterol	25.7 mg
Sodium	320.4 mg
Carbohydrates	25.1 g
Protein	10.4 g

Ingredients

Dough
3 C. all-purpose flour
1 tsp. salt
1/2 tsp. baking powder
1/2 tsp. baking soda
1/4 C. vegetable oil
1 C. warm water
Filling
1 lb. browned ground beef
1/2 medium onion, diced

1/2 green bell pepper, diced
3 garlic cloves, crushed
1/8 C. chopped fresh cilantro
1/8 C. sliced green olives
1 pinch salt and pepper
1 tbsp. tomato paste
1 (1 1/4 oz.) packages sazon goya with coriander and annatto
For Frying
1 C. vegetable oil

Directions

1. For the dough: in a bowl, add the flour, baking powder, baking soda and salt and mix well.
2. Add the oil and water and with an electric mixer, mix until a dough forms.
3. Place the dough onto a lightly floured surface and with your hands, knead for about 3 minutes.
4. With a plastic wrap, cover the dough for about 15 minutes.
5. Place the dough onto a lightly floured surface and cut into 12 equal sized pieces.
6. Now, roll each piece into a 4-inch circle.
7. For the filling: in a skillet, add the ground beef and cook until browned completely, breaking up the meat.
8. Drain the grease from the beef.
9. Stir in the remaining ingredients and cook for about 10 minutes, mixing often.
10. Remove from the heat and keep aside to cool.
11. Place about 2 tbsp. of the filling onto each dough circle.

12. Fold the dough over the filling and press the edges to seal.
13. In a skillet, add the oil over medium heat and cook until heated through.
14. Add the empanadas in batches and cook for about 10 minutes, flipping once half way through.
15. With a slotted spoon, transfer the empanadas onto a paper towels-lined plate to drain.
16. Enjoy warm.

EMPANADAS
Ciudad

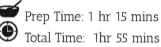

Prep Time: 1 hr 15 mins
Total Time: 1hr 55 mins

Servings per Recipe: 12
Calories	306.8 kcal
Fat	20.0 g
Cholesterol	118.8 mg
Sodium	387.5 mg
Carbohydrates	18.2 g
Protein	12.8 g

Ingredients

Dough
2 C. all-purpose flour, sifted
1-2 tsp. salt
3/4 C. cold margarine, small cubes
2 eggs
2/3 C. cold water
2 tbsp. white vinegar
Filling
1 lb. ground beef

4 hard-boiled eggs, peeled and chopped
1 C. stuffed green olive, halved
handful raisins
1 large onion, minced
3 garlic cloves, minced
2-3 tbsp. ground cumin powder
1 tsp. chili pepper flakes
salt and pepper

Directions

1. In a bowl, add the flour and salt and mix well.
2. With a pastry blender, cut in the margarine until coarse crumb like mixture forms.
3. In another bowl, add the eggs, vinegar and water and beat until well combined.
4. Slowly, add the egg mixture into the flour mixture and mix until a sticky dough forms.
5. Place the dough onto a floured surface and with your hands, knead well.
6. With a plastic wrap, cover the dough and keep in a cool place for about 2 hours.
7. Now, roll the dough into 1/8-inch thickness.
8. Then, cut the rolled dough into 4-6-inch circles.
9. In a pot, add the oil and cook until heated through.
10. Add the onions and garlic and cook for about 4-5 minutes.
11. Add the ground beef and cook until meat is no more pink, break up with a spoon.
12. Drain the grease from the beef.
13. Stir in the sugar, cumin and chili pepper flakes and remove from the heat.

14. Add the olives, eggs, salt and pepper and gently, stir to combine.
15. Set your oven to 375 degrees F and grease a baking sheet.
16. Place about 2-3 tbsp. of the filling onto the center of each dough circle.
17. With wet fingers, moisten the edges of each circle.
18. Fold the dough over the filling and press the edges to seal.
19. In the bottom of the prepared baking sheet, arrange the empanadas.
20. Cook in the oven for about 15-20 minutes.
21. Enjoy warm.

MIAMI
Steak Empanadas with Cheese Sauce

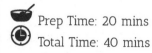

Prep Time: 20 mins
Total Time: 40 mins

Servings per Recipe: 4
Calories	1279.9 kcal
Fat	98.2 g
Cholesterol	135.5 mg
Sodium	1063.9 mg
Carbohydrates	64.0 g
Protein	36.3 g

Ingredients

1/2 lb. steak, diced into 1/4-inch bite-size chunks
1/2 tsp. Cajun spices
1/2 tsp. oregano
1/2 tsp. cumin
1/4 tsp. salt
1/4 tsp. black pepper
2 tbsp. olive oil
1/4 C. onion, diced
2 garlic cloves, minced
1/4 C. green bell pepper, diced
2 Serrano peppers, minced
1/4 C. salsa

2 tbsp. beef broth
1 tbsp. tomato paste
1 C. Monterey Jack cheese, shredded
2 puff pastry sheets, thawed
1/4 C. butter, melted
Sauce
1 tbsp. butter, unsalted
1 tbsp. flour
1 C. milk
1 C. Monterey jJack cheese, shredded
1/2 tsp. cumin
salt and pepper, to taste

Directions

1. In a bowl, add the steak cubes, oregano, Cajun spices, cumin, salt and black pepper and toss to cot well.
2. In a skillet, add the oil and cook until heated.
3. Add the peppers, onions and garlic and stir fry for about 4-5 minutes.
4. Add the steak and cook until done completely.
5. In a bowl, add the salsa, tomato paste and broth and mix well.
6. In the steak mixture, add the salsa mixture and cook for about 1-2 minutes.
7. Stir in the cheese and remove from the heat.
8. Transfer the steak mixture into a bowl and refrigerate until using.
9. Set your oven to 400 degrees F before doing anything else and grease a baking sheet.

10. Cut 9 equal sized squares from each pastry sheet.
11. Place about 1-2 tbsp. of the steak mixture onto each square.
12. With wet fingers, moisten the edges of each circle.
13. Fold the dough over the filling in a triangle and press the edges to seal.
14. In the bottom of the prepared baking sheet, arrange the empanadas.
15. Coat each empanada with the melted butter and with a fork, pierce the top.
16. Cook in the oven for about 15-20 minutes.
17. Meanwhile, in a frying pan, add the butter over medium heat and cook until melted.
18. Add the flour, beating continuously and cook for about 1 minute.
19. Slowly, add the milk, beating continuously until well combined.
20. Slowly, add the cheese, mixing continuously until melted.
21. Stir in the cumin, salt and pepper and remove from the heat.
22. Enjoy the empanadas warm with a drizzling of the cheese sauce.

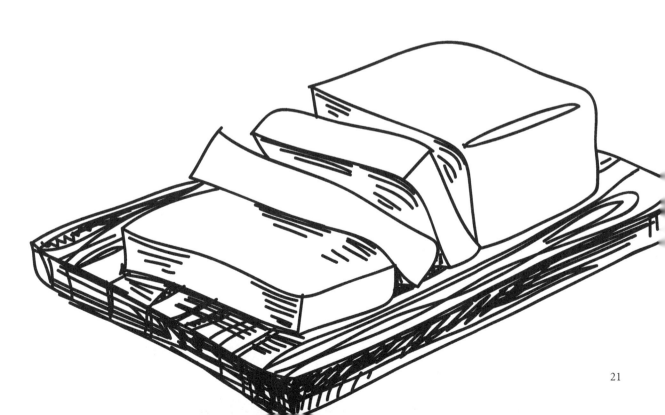

ROASTED
Empanadas

Prep Time: 45 mins
Total Time: 1 hr 15 mins

Servings per Recipe: 1	
Calories	37.8 kcal
Fat	0.4 g
Cholesterol	4.5 mg
Sodium	91.2 mg
Carbohydrates	5.9 g
Protein	2.3 g

Ingredients

1 C. finely chopped red potatoes
1 C. finely chopped onion
1 C. beef broth
1/4 tsp. salt
1/4 tsp. ground cumin
1/4 tsp. ground allspice
1/4 tsp. black pepper
1/2 lb. boneless beef top sirloin steak,

trimmed and diced
1 garlic clove, minced
1 tbsp. finely chopped cilantro
1 tbsp. cornstarch
1 tbsp. cold water
36 wonton wrappers
cooking spray
fresh cilantro stem

Directions

1. In a pot, add the beef, potatoes, onion, garlic, cilantro, beef broth, cumin, allspice, salt and black pepper over medium heat and cook for about 8 minutes, mixing often.
2. Set the heat to low and cook for about 8 minutes, mixing often.
3. Remove from the heat and keep aside to cool completely.
4. Set your oven to 400 degrees F and arrange 2 baking sheets in the oven for about 10 minutes.
5. In a colander, drain the beef mixture completely, discarding the liquid.
6. In a food processor, add the beef mixture and pulse until finely chopped.
7. Meanwhile, in a bowl, add the cornstarch and water and beat until well combined.
8. Place about 1 tbsp. of the beef mixture onto the center of each wonton wrapper.
9. Coat the edges of each wonton wrapper with the cornstarch mixture.
10. Fold the dough over the filling and press the edges to seal.
11. In the bottom of the pre-heated baking sheets, arrange the empanadas and spray with the cooking spray.
12. Cook in the oven for about 4 minutes per side.
13. Enjoy warm with a garnishing of the cilantro.

Central
American Chili Empanadas

🥣 Prep Time: 15 mins
🕐 Total Time:: 40 mins

Servings per Recipe: 12
Calories	271.1 kcal
Fat	19.2 g
Cholesterol	19.2 mg
Sodium	225.2 mg
Carbohydrates	17.3 g
Protein	6.9 g

Ingredients

1 (15 oz.) boxes pillsbury ready-made pie crusts
3/4 lb. ground beef
1 medium onion, diced
1 small bell pepper, diced
1 bay leaf
2 garlic cloves, diced

4 tbsp. oil
1/2 tsp. oregano
1/4 C. chopped green chili pepper

Directions

1. Set your oven to 400 degrees F before doing anything else and grease a baking sheet.
2. For the filling: in a skillet, add the oil and cook until heated.
3. Add the beef and cook until meat is no more pink.
4. Drain the grease from the beef.
5. stir in the remaining ingredients and cook, covered for about 30 minutes.
6. Remove from the heat and discard the bay leaf.
7. For the crust: place the dough onto a lightly floured surface and roll into 1/8-inch thickness.
8. With a cookie cutter, cut the circles from the dough.
9. Place about 1/2 tsp. of the filling onto each circle.
10. Fold the dough over the filling and press the edges to seal.
11. In the bottom of the prepared baking sheet, arrange the empanadas and coat the top of each with the beaten egg.
12. Cook in the oven until golden brown.
13. Enjoy warm.

LUNCH
Box Empanadas

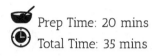

Prep Time: 20 mins
Total Time: 35 mins

Servings per Recipe: 6
Calories   318.4 kcal
Fat   18.1 g
Cholesterol   39.7m g
Sodium   1069.9 mg
Carbohydrates   24.6 g
Protein   15.6 g

Ingredients

2 tbsp. olive oil
1 lb. refrigerated pizza dough
1/2 C. flour
1 (16 oz.) cans refried beans
1 (1 pint) container fresh salsa
1 (8 oz.) packages shredded cheddar
cheese

sour cream
avocado

Directions

1. Set your oven to 400 degrees F before doing anything else and grease a baking sheet with 1 tsp. of the oil.
2. Place the dough onto a lightly floured surface and cut into 6 equal sized pieces.
3. Now, roll each piece into a 8-inch circle.
4. Place the beans onto each circle evenly, followed by the salsa and cheese.
5. Fold the dough over the filling and press the edges to seal.
6. In the bottom of the prepared baking sheet, arrange the empanadas and coat the top of each with the remaining oil.
7. Cook in the oven for about 12-15 minutes.
8. Enjoy warm with a topping of the sour cream and avocado.

Catalina's
Catalina's

Servings per Recipe: 6

Calories	163.7 kcal
Fat	10.6 g
Cholesterol	81.1 mg
Sodium	202.6 mg
Carbohydrates	2.9 g
Protein	13.5 g

Ingredients

1 1/2 C. chopped cooked chicken
1/2 C. shredded Swiss cheese
2 tbsp. chopped roasted red peppers
2 tbsp. minced onions
1/2 tsp. pepper
1/2 C. chicken broth
1 tbsp. cornstarch

1 (3 oz.) packages cream cheese, small chunks
salt
2 (10 oz.) packages refrigerated pizza dough
1 large egg, beaten

Directions

1. Set your oven to 375 degrees F before doing anything else and grease a 12x15-inch baking sheet.
2. In a bowl, add the Swiss cheese, chicken, onion, red pepper and black pepper and mix until well combined.
3. In a pot, add the broth and cornstarch over high heat and beat until well combined.
4. Add the cream cheese and cook for about 2-3 minutes, beating continuously.
5. Pour the cheese mixture over the chicken mixture alongside the salt and stir to combine well.
6. Place the dough onto a lightly floured surface and unroll it.
7. Cut each rectangle into thirds crosswise.
8. Place about 5 tbsp. of the chicken mixture dough piece.
9. Fold the dough over the filling in a rectangle shape and press the edges to seal.
10. In the bottom of the prepared baking sheet, arrange the empanadas and coat each with the beaten egg.
11. Cook in the oven for about 22-25 minutes.
12. Enjoy warm.

COCKTAIL
Empanadas

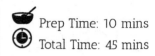 Prep Time: 10 mins
Total Time: 45 mins

Servings per Recipe: 1

Calories	114.4 kcal
Fat	7.1 g
Cholesterol	9.6 mg
Sodium	124.0 mg
Carbohydrates	8.7 g
Protein	3.7 g

Ingredients

2 pie crusts
3/4 lb. ground beef
1 medium onion, chopped
1 1/4 oz. taco seasoning
2 garlic cloves, minced
1 green pepper, chopped
1 C. Clamato juice

Directions

1. In a nonstick pan, add the ground beef and onions over medium-high heat and cook until browned.
2. Stir in the garlic, seasoning packet, green pepper and Clamato and cook for about 10 minutes, mixing occasionally.
3. Remove from the heat and keep aside to cool.
4. Set your oven to 350 degrees F before doing anything else and grease a baking sheet.
5. Cut 12 (3-inch) circles from the pie crust.
6. Place the mixture on the center of each round evenly.
7. Fold the dough over the filling and press the edges to seal.
8. In the bottom of the prepared baking sheet, arrange the empanadas.
9. Cook in the oven for about 15-20 minutes.
10. Enjoy warm.

Mi Tia's Empanadas

Prep Time: 15 mins
Total Time: 35 mins

Servings per Recipe: 1	
Calories	79.3 kcal
Fat	3.4 g
Cholesterol	9.3 mg
Sodium	28.0 mg
Carbohydrates	11.6 g
Protein	0.6 g

Ingredients

4 oz. butter, softened
3 oz. cream cheese
5 oz. plain flour
11 oz. fruit jam
3 oz. superfine sugar
1/2 tsp. ground cinnamon

Directions

1. In a bowl, add the cream cheese and butter and beat until well smooth.
2. Add the flour and beat until well combined.
3. Make a smooth ball from the dough.
4. With a cling film, cover the dough ball and refrigerate for about 8 hours.
5. Remove from the refrigerator and keep aside at room temperature for about 20 minutes.
6. Set your oven to 375 degrees F.
7. Place the dough ball onto a lightly floured surface and roll into a 1/4-inch thickness.
8. With a 3-inch biscuit cutter, cut the rolled dough into circles.
9. Place a small spoon of the jam onto the center of each circle.
10. With wet fingers, moisten the edges of each circle.
11. Fold the dough over the filling and press the edges to seal.
12. In the bottom of an ungreased baking sheet, arrange the empanadas.
13. Cook in the oven for about 15-20 minutes.
14. Meanwhile, in a bowl, add the sugar and cinnamon and mix well.
15. Remove the empanadas from the oven and immediately, coat each with the cinnamon sugar.
16. Enjoy warm.

SATURDAY
Night Chicken Empanadas

Prep Time: 40 mins
Total Time: 1 hr

Servings per Recipe: 12
Calories	285.4 kcal
Fat	19.7 g
Cholesterol	22.4 mg
Sodium	732.3 mg
Carbohydrates	20.9 g
Protein	6.3 g

Ingredients

3 C. chicken, cooked and chopped
1 (8 oz.) packages shredded cheese
4 oz. cream cheese, softened
1 red bell pepper, chopped
1 jalapeño, seeded and chopped
1 tbsp. ground cumin
1 1/2 tsp. salt

1/2 tsp. ground black pepper
1 (15 oz.) packages refrigerated pie crusts
water
Sauce
1 C. Velveeta cheese
1 C. tomatoes, diced

Directions

1. In a bowl, add the chicken, cream cheese, cheese blend, jalapeño, red pepper, cumin, salt and pepper and mix well.
2. Place each pie crust onto a lightly floured surface and then, roll each into a 15-inch circle.
3. With a 3-inch cookie cutter, cut the circles.
4. Place 1 heaping tsp. of the chicken mixture onto the center of each dough circle.
5. With wet fingers, moisten the edges of each circle.
6. Fold the dough over the filling and press the edges to seal.
7. In a deep skillet, add the vegetable oil and cook until its temperature reaches to 350 degrees F.
8. Add the empanadas in batches and cook for about 3-5 minutes.
9. For the sauce: in a pan, add the cheese over medium-low heat and cook until melted completely.
10. Add tomatoes and mix until blended nicely.
11. With a slotted spoon, transfer the empanadas onto a paper towel-lined plate to drain.
12. Enjoy warm alongside the cheese dip.

Rancho
Empanadas

🥣 Prep Time: 1 hrs
🕐 Total Time: 1 hr 10 mins

Servings per Recipe: 16
Calories	480.6 kcal
Fat	32.5 g
Cholesterol	68.9 mg
Sodium	195.7 mg
Carbohydrates	35.9 g
Protein	11.6 g

Ingredients

Empanadas
1 tbsp. olive oil
1/2 lb. ground beef
3 large garlic cloves, chopped
1 tbsp. tomato paste
1 tsp. ground cumin
1/4 tsp. cayenne pepper
1/3 C. chopped fresh cilantro
salt and pepper

1 ½ packages frozen puff pastry, thawed,
approx. 3 sheets
3 large egg yolks, beaten, glaze
Sauce
1 (15 oz.) cans black beans, drained
1 C. sour cream
2 Roma tomatoes, chopped, separated
2 large scallions, chopped, separated
salt and pepper

Directions

1. In a skillet, add the oil over medium-high heat and cook until heated through.
2. Add the beef and garlic and cook for about 3 minutes, breaking up the meat.
3. Add the tomato paste, cayenne and cumin and stir to combine.
4. Set the heat to medium and cook for about 4 minutes, mixing occasionally.
5. Stir in the cilantro, salt and pepper and remove from the heat.
6. Keep aside to cool completely.
7. Set your oven to 375 degrees F and line 2 baking sheets with the parchment paper.
8. Cut each pastry sheet into 4 (4 1/2-inch) squares.
9. Coat each square with a thin layer of beaten eggs.
10. Place the filling onto center of each dough square evenly.
11. Fold the dough over the filling to form triangle and press the edges to seal.
12. In the bottom of the prepared baking sheets, arrange the empanadas and coat the top of each with the beaten eggs.
13. Cook in the oven for about 20 minutes.

14. Meanwhile, in a food processor, add the sour cream and beans and pulse until smooth.
15. Transfer the beans puree into a bowl.
16. Add 1/2 of the scallions, 1/2 of the tomatoes, salt and pepper and stir to combine.
17. Enjoy the empanadas warm with a garnishing of the remaining tomatoes and scallions alongside the beans mixture.

Empanadas
Bolivia

Prep Time: 35 mins
Total Time: 1 hr

Servings per Recipe: 12

Calories	202.3 kcal
Fat	13.3 g
Cholesterol	34.6 mg
Sodium	187.8 mg
Carbohydrates	15.3 g
Protein	5.5 g

Ingredients

1 tbsp. olive oil
1 small onion, chopped
1/2 lb. ground beef
1/3 C. golden raisin
2 tbsp. ketchup
1/4 tsp. ground cinnamon
kosher salt and black pepper

2 store-bought refrigerated rolled pie crusts
1 large egg, beaten
1/2 C. sour cream
1/4 tsp. lime zest

Directions

1. Set your oven to 375 degrees F before doing anything else and grease a baking sheet.
2. In a skillet, add the oil over medium heat and cook until heated through.
3. Add the onion and cook for about 5-6 minutes, mixing often.
4. Add the beef and cook for about 3-4 minutes, breaking up the meat.
5. Stir in the ketchup, raisins, cinnamon, 1/2 tsp. of the salt and 1/4 tsp. of the pepper and remove from the heat.
6. With a 2 1/2-inch round cookie cutter, cut the circles from the dough.
7. Place the beef mixture onto each circle evenly.
8. With wet fingers, moisten the edges of each circle.
9. Fold the dough over the filling and press the edges to seal.
10. In the bottom of the prepared baking sheet, arrange the empZanadas and coat each with the beaten egg.
11. Cook in the oven for about 20-25 minutes.
12. Meanwhile, in a bowl, add the sour cream and lime zest and mix.
13. Enjoy the empanadas warm alongside the sour cream.

MY
First Empanada

Prep Time: 1 hr
Total Time: 1 hr 15 mins

Servings per Recipe: 8
Calories	235.0 kcal
Fat	11.6 g
Cholesterol	73.7 mg
Sodium	233.2 mg
Carbohydrates	8.5 g
Protein	23.1 g

Ingredients

2 lb. lean ground beef
1 large onion, chopped
4 garlic cloves, minced
2 tsp. cinnamon
1/2 tsp. cumin
1/2 tsp. coriander
1/2 tsp. clove

1 tbsp. chili powder
3 tbsp. brown sugar
1 tbsp. vinegar
1/2 tsp. salt
1 tsp. chile, crushed
pepper
pastry dough

Directions

1. In a nonstick skillet, add the beef, onion and garlic over medium heat and cook until meat is browned.
2. Stir in the remaining ingredients and cook for about 15 minutes.
3. Remove from the heat and keep aside to cool completely.
4. Set your oven to 350 degrees F.
5. Place the pastry onto a lightly floured surface and roll into 1/8-inch thickness.
6. Then, cut the rolled dough into 3-inch circles.
7. Place a spoonful of the filling onto each dough circle.
8. With wet fingers, moisten the edges of each circle.
9. Fold the dough over the filling and press the edges to seal.
10. In the bottom of an ungreased baking sheet, arrange the empanadas.
11. With a fork, prick the top of each empanada.
12. Cook in the oven for about 20 minutes.
13. Enjoy warm.

Seattle
Empanadas

🥣 Prep Time: 45 mins
🕐 Total Time: 57 mins

Servings per Recipe: 1
Calories	90.0 kcal
Fat	6.6 g
Cholesterol	22.3 mg
Sodium	105.6 mg
Carbohydrates	5.6 g
Protein	2.1 g

Ingredients

Pastry
2 (8 oz.) packages cream cheese, softened
3/4 C. butter, softened
2 1/2 C. flour
1/2 tsp. salt
Filling
1/4 C. finely chopped onion
3 garlic cloves, minced
5 slices turkey bacon, cooked and
crumbled, drippings saved
1 (10 oz.) packages frozen chopped spinach,
thawed and drained
1 C. small curd cottage cheese
1/4 tsp. pepper
1/8 tsp. nutmeg
1 egg, for egg wash
salsa, for serving

Directions

1. For the dough: in a bowl, add the butter and cream cheese and beat until smooth.
2. Slowly, add the flour and salt, beating continuously until well combined.
3. Now, with your hands, knead well.
4. With a plastic wrap, cover the dough and refrigerate for about 3 hours.
5. For the filling: in a skillet, add the reserved bacon grease and cook until heated.
6. Add the onion and garlic and stir fry for about 3-4 minutes.
7. Stir in the spinach, crumbled bacon, cottage cheese, nutmeg and pepper and remove from the heat.
8. Keep aside to cool completely.
9. Set your oven to 450 degrees F.
10. Place the pastry onto a lightly floured surface and unroll it.
11. Then, roll the pastry into 1/8-inch thickness.
12. With a 3-inch cookie cutter, cut the circles from the pastry.
13. Place about 1 tsp. of the filling onto one half of each circle.

14. Coat the edges of circle with the egg wash.
15. Fold the dough over the filling and press the edges to seal.
16. In the bottom of an ungreased baking sheet, arrange the empanadas.
17. Cook in the oven for about 10-12 minutes.
18. Enjoy warm.

Empanadas
in Argentina

🥣 Prep Time: 45 mins
🕐 Total Time: 1 hr 5 mins

Servings per Recipe: 1	
Calories	471.9 kcal
Fat	32.0 g
Cholesterol	46.0 mg
Sodium	353.1 mg
Carbohydrates	34.4 g
Protein	11.5 g

Ingredients

Filling
2 tsp. olive oil
1 lb. ground beef
2 medium boiling potatoes, peeled, boiled
15 minutes, grated
1 large onion, finely chopped
3/4 tsp. ground red chili powder
1/2 tsp. ground cumin
salt & freshly ground black pepper
Dough
3 1/2 C. all-purpose flour
2 tsp. baking powder

1 tsp. salt
1/2 C. butter, cut into pieces
1/2 C. vegetable shortening
5-6 tbsp. cold water
Chimichuri
1/2 C. olive oil
1/4 C. minced fresh parsley
2 tbsp. fresh lemon juice
1 large shallot, minced
1 medium garlic clove, minced
1 tsp. minced fresh herb
salt & freshly ground black pepper

Directions

1. For the chimichuri sauce: in a bowl, add all the ingredients and mix well.
2. Cover the bowl and keep aside for about 3 hours.
3. For the filling: in a skillet, add the oil over medium heat and cook until heated through.
4. Add the crumbled beef and cook for about 4 minutes.
5. Add the onion, potatoes, cumin, chili powder, salt and pepper and stir fry for about 5 minutes.
6. Remove from the heat and keep aside to cool completely.
7. For the dough: in a bowl, add the flour, baking powder and salt and mix well.
8. With a pastry blender, cut in the shortening and butter until coarse meal like mixture forms.
9. Add enough water and mix until a dough ball forms.
10. Now, with your hands, knead until a smooth dough forms.

11. Keep aside for about 15 minutes.
12. Set your oven to 400 degrees F.
13. Place the dough onto a lightly floured surface and roll into 1/8-inch thickness.
14. Cut the rolled dough into 5 1/2-inch circles.
15. Place 2 tbsp. of the filling onto the center of each circle.
16. Fold the dough over the filling and press the edges to seal.
17. In the bottom of an ungreased baking sheet, arrange the empanadas.
18. With a fork, prick the top of each empanada.
19. Cook in the oven for about 15-20 minutes.
20. Enjoy hot alongside the chimichuri sauce.

Empanadas
Marrakech

🍳 Prep Time: 15 mins
🕐 Total Time: 35 mins

Servings per Recipe: 1	
Calories	380.2 kcal
Fat	23.2 g
Cholesterol	24.0 mg
Sodium	159.3 mg
Carbohydrates	31.8 g
Protein	11.0 g

Ingredients

1 lb. lamb (leg), small cubes
2 sheets puff pastry sheets, thawed
1 medium onion, chopped
1 large potato, peeled and chopped
3 medium carrots, peeled and chopped
1 small turnip, peeled and chopped
salt and pepper, to taste

Directions

1. Set your oven to 400 degrees F before doing anything else and line a baking sheet with the parchment paper.
2. In a bowl, add all the ingredients except the pastry and mix well.
3. Place the pastry sheets onto a lightly floured surface and separate them.
4. With a 5 1/2-inch saucer, cut the circles from the pastry.
5. Place a heaping tsp. of the lamb mixture in the center of each pastry circle.
6. With wet fingers, moisten the edges of each circle.
7. Fold the dough over the filling and press the edges to seal.
8. In the bottom of the prepared baking sheet, arrange the empanadas.
9. Cook in the oven for about 15-20 minutes.
10. Enjoy warm.

CHEDDAR
Chicken
Empanadas

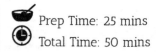 Prep Time: 25 mins
Total Time: 50 mins

Servings per Recipe: 15
Calories	155.4 kcal
Fat	9.5 g
Cholesterol	30.5 mg
Sodium	85.0 mg
Carbohydrates	11.4 g
Protein	6.1 g

Ingredients

1 1/2 C. diced cooked chicken
2 granny smith apples, peeled and
chopped
1 tsp. thyme
1 tbsp. honey
1 tbsp. butter
1/2 small white onion

1 garlic clove, minced
1/2 C. shredded cheddar cheese
salt and pepper
1 sheet puff pastry
1 egg, beaten

Directions

1. Set your oven to 400 degrees F before doing anything else and grease a baking sheet.
2. In a skillet, add the butter and cook until melted completely.
3. Add the apple, onion and garlic and stir fry until tender.
4. Stir in the chicken, honey, thyme, salt and pepper and remove from the heat.
5. Keep aside to cool slightly.
6. Add the cheddar cheese and stir to combine.
7. Place the puff pastry onto a lightly floured surface and roll into 1/8-inch thickness.
8. With a glass, cut the circles from the pastry.
9. Place about 1 tbsp. of the filling onto each circle.
10. Fold the dough over the filling and press the edges to seal.
11. In the bottom of the prepared baking sheet, arrange the empanadas and coat each with the egg wash.
12. Cook in the oven for about 25 minutes.
13. Enjoy warm.

Empanadas
Buena Caritas

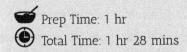 Prep Time: 1 hr
Total Time: 1 hr 28 mins

Servings per Recipe: 1
Calories	391.3 kcal
Fat	27.0 g
Cholesterol	43.0 mg
Sodium	475.7 mg
Carbohydrates	24.8 g
Protein	12.0 g

Ingredients

Dough
4 C. all-purpose flour
4 tsp. baking powder
2 tsp. curry powder
1 tsp. salt
1 tsp. turmeric
1 1/3 C. shortening
1/2 C. butter
1 C. cold water
Filling
2 tbsp. vegetable oil

2 medium onions, finely chopped
2 garlic cloves, minced
2 lb. ground beef
1 tbsp. curry powder
1 1/2 tsp. salt
1 1/2 tsp. dried thyme
1 tsp. black pepper
1 pinch cayenne pepper
2 C. water
1 C. plain breadcrumbs

Directions

1. For the dough: in a bowl, add the flour, baking powder, turmeric, curry powder and salt and mix well.
2. With a pastry blender, cut in the shortening and butter until a fine crumb like mixture forms.
3. Add the water and mix until a soft dough forms.
4. Make a ball from the dough.
5. With a wax paper, cover the dough ball and refrigerate for about 1 hour.
6. For the filling: in a bowl, add the breadcrumbs and water and mix well.
7. Keep aside until using.
8. In a pot, add the oil over medium heat and cook until heated through.
9. Add the onions and garlic and stir fry for about 3-4 minutes.
10. Transfer the onion mixture into a bowl and keep aside.

11. In the same pot, add the beef over high heat and cook until browned.
12. Drain the grease from the beef.
13. Add the onion mixture, thyme, curry powder, cayenne pepper, salt and black pepper and stir to combine.
14. Set the heat to medium and cook for about 3 minutes.
15. Remove from the heat and keep aside.
16. Set your oven to 350 degrees F and grease a baking sheet.
17. Place the dough onto a lightly floured surface and cut into 12 equal sized pieces.
18. Now, roll each piece into a 6-inch circle.
19. Place the filling onto each circle evenly.
20. With wet fingers, moisten the edges of each circle.
21. Fold the dough over the filling and press the edges to seal.
22. In the bottom of the prepared baking sheet, arrange the empanadas.
23. Cook in the oven for about 28 minutes.
24. Enjoy warm.

Southwest
Yam Empanadas with White Sauce

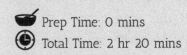 Prep Time: 0 mins

Total Time: 2 hr 20 mins

Servings per Recipe: 16
Calories	484.9 kcal
Fat	20.8 g
Cholesterol	104.6 mg
Sodium	980.4 mg
Carbohydrates	61.4 g
Protein	13.4 g

Ingredients

Dough
4 C. all-purpose flour, plus additional for rolling dough
4 tsp. kosher salt
1 C. unsalted butter, cold and cubed
2 large eggs
2 tbsp. white vinegar
1/3-2/3 C. cold water
Filling
1/2 tsp. chili powder
1/2 tsp. ground coriander
1/2 tsp. ground cumin
2 jalapeños, stemmed, seeded and finely

diced
3-4 medium sweet potatoes, cooked and mashed
2 (15 oz.) cans black beans, rinsed and drained
kosher salt
White Sauce
1 C. Greek yogurt
3 tbsp. lemon juice plus 1 tbsp. lemon zest
1 tbsp. chopped fresh cilantro
1 tsp. ground cumin
kosher salt
Egg Wash
1 large egg, lightly beaten

Directions

1. For the dough: in a food processor, add the flour and salt.
2. Add the butter and process until a coarse meal like mixture is formed.
3. Add the eggs, vinegar, and 1/3-2/3 C. of the cold water and process until just a dough forms.
4. Place the dough onto a smooth surface and with your hands, pat it into a flat disk.
5. With a plastic wrap, wrap the dough disc tightly and place in the fridge for about 1 hour.
6. For the filling: in a dry skillet, add the coriander, cumin and chile powder and stir fry until just aromatic.
7. Stir in the beans, sweet potatoes, jalapeños and salt and remove from the heat.
8. For the white sauce: in a bowl, add all the ingredients and mix until well combined.

9. Cover the bowl and place in the fridge until using.
10. Set your oven to 400 degrees F and grease a baking sheet.
11. Make 10 equal sized balls from the dough.
12. Place the balls onto a floured surface and roll each into a 6-inch round.
13. Place about 3-4 tbsp. of the filling onto the center of each dough round.
14. Coat the edges of each round with the egg wash.
15. Fold the dough over the filling and press the edges to seal.
16. In the bottom of the prepared baking sheet, arrange the empanadas and coat the top of each with egg wash.
17. Cook in the oven for about 25 minutes.
18. Enjoy warm alongside the white sauce.

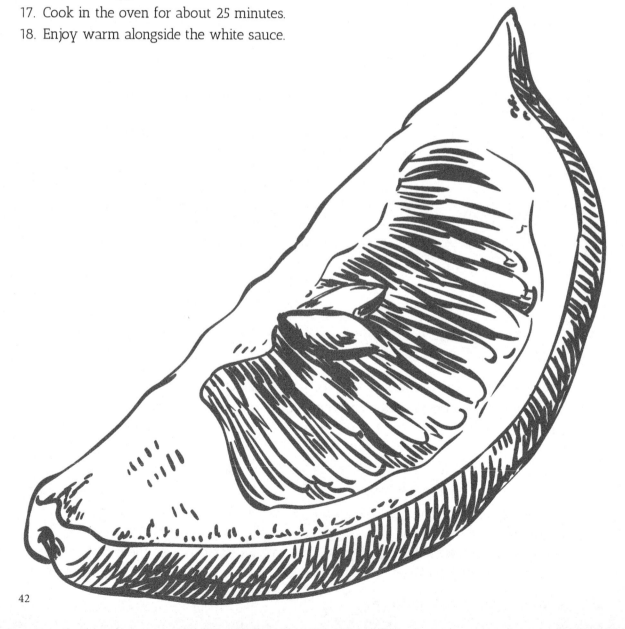

Elizabeth's
Empanadas

Prep Time: 0 mins

Total Time: 3 hrs 45 mins

Servings per Recipe: 16	
Calories	597.8 kcal
Fat	36.0 g
Cholesterol	139.1 mg
Sodium	227.3 mg
Carbohydrates	61.9 g
Protein	8.7 g

Ingredients

1 large egg, beaten
2-3 tbsp. unsalted butter
3 large apples, cored, peeled, diced
1 dash turbinado sugar
3 tbsp. brown sugar
1 tsp. ground cinnamon
1 pinch salt
bench flour, for dusting
almond pastry

1 (17 1/3 oz.) boxes frozen puff pastry, thawed
Almond Pastry Crème
1 1/2 C. whole milk
1/2 C. sugar
2 tbsp. almond paste
1 pinch salt
4 large egg yolks
2 tbsp. cornstarch
3 tbsp. unsalted butter

Directions

1. For the almond pastry cream: in a heavy-bottomed pot, add the milk, almond paste, sugar and salt over medium heat and beat until well combined.
2. Cook until just boiling, mixing continuously.
3. In a bowl, add the egg yolks and cornstarch. And beat until thick and creamy.
4. Remove the milk mixture from the heat.
5. Slowly, add 1/4 C. of the milk mixture into the egg mixture, beating continuously until well combined.
6. Add the egg mixture into the pot of the remaining milk mixture and stir to combine.
7. Place the pan over the heat and cook for about 3 minutes, beating continuously.
8. Remove from the heat and stir in the butter until well combined.
9. Through a sieve, strain the pastry cream into a bowl.
10. Arrange a plastic wrap directly onto the surface of pastry cream and place in the fridge for about 3 hours.
11. In a skillet, add the butter over medium heat and cook until melted completely.

12. Add the apples and stir fry for about 5 minutes.
13. Add the brown sugar, salt and cinnamon and cook for about 10 minutes, mixing often.
14. Remove from the heat and with a fork, mash the mixture until a chunky applesauce like mixture forms.
15. Keep aside to cool completely.
16. Set your oven to 400 degrees F and line a baking sheet with the parchment paper.
17. After cooling of the apple mixture, gently fold in 1/4 C. of the pastry cream.
18. Place the puff pastry sheets onto a floured surface and separate them.
19. With a 4 1/2-inch round biscuit cutter, cut 4 large circles from each pastry sheet.
20. Place about 2 heaping tbsp. of the apple mixture onto the bottom half of each dough circle.
21. Coat the edges of each pastry circle with the egg wash.
22. Fold the dough over the filling and press the edges to seal.
23. In the bottom of the prepared baking sheet, arrange the empanadas.
24. With a knife, make 2 slits on top of each empanada.
25. Coat each empanada with the remaining egg wash and dust with the turbinado sugar.
26. Cook in the oven for about 20 minutes.
27. Remove from the oven and enjoy with the topping of the remaining almond pastry cream.

Punta
Cana Empanadas

Prep Time: 15 mins
Total Time: 35 mins

Servings per Recipe: 7
Calories	371.9 kcal
Fat	20.3 g
Cholesterol	35.6 mg
Sodium	544.2 mg
Carbohydrates	32.2 g
Protein	15.5 g

Ingredients

2 C. roasted chicken meat, shredded
1 C. whole kernel corn
1/4 C. golden raisin
2 tbsp. fresh cilantro, chopped
2 tbsp. onions, minced
1/4-1/2 C. crumbled goat cheese
1/2 tsp. kosher salt

1/4 tsp. black pepper, freshly ground
2 (9 inch) pie crusts

Directions

1. Set your oven to 375 degrees F before doing anything else and line a baking sheet with the parchment paper.
2. In a large bowl, add the chicken, cheese, raisins, corn, onion, cilantro, salt and pepper and mix well.
3. With a 2-inch biscuit cutter, cut an rounds from each pie crust.
4. Place the chicken mixture onto half of each round evenly, leaving a little edge.
5. With wet fingers, moisten the edges of each circle.
6. Fold the dough over the filling and press the edges to seal.
7. In the bottom of the prepared baking sheet, arrange the empanadas.
8. With a fork, poke the top of each empanada.
9. Cook in the oven for about 20 minutes.
10. Enjoy warm.

EMPANADAS
Colombiana

Prep Time: 30 mins
Total Time: 50 mins

Servings per Recipe: 8
Calories	358.0 kcal
Fat	18.4 g
Cholesterol	91.4 mg
Sodium	542.0 mg
Carbohydrates	40.0 g
Protein	8.1 g

Ingredients

Dough
3 C. flour
2 tsp. baking powder
3/4 tsp. salt
1/3 C. butter
2 eggs
1/3 C. milk
1 egg, beaten
Filling
1 large onion, minced

1 red jalapeño chile, minced
1 green jalapeño, minced
1 tomatoes, minced
1 green onion, minced
2 tbsp. parsley, chopped
2 garlic cloves, minced
1/2 C. green olives, chopped
1/4 C. vegetable oil
3 C. queso fresco, crumbled

Directions

1. Set your oven to 350 degrees F before doing anything else and grease a baking sheet.
2. In a skillet, add the oil and cook until heated through.
3. Add the remaining ingredients except the cheese and cook for about 10 minutes, mixing frequently.
4. Remove from the heat and stir in the cheese.
5. Meanwhile, for the dough: in a bowl, add the flour, baking powder and salt and mix well.
6. With a pastry blender, cut in the butter until a coarse meal like mixture forms.
7. Add the eggs and milk and mix until a smooth dough forms.
8. Place the dough onto a lightly floured surface and roll very thinly.
9. With a round cutter, cut the dough into circles.
10. Place the filling onto the center half of dough circles evenly, leaving border.
11. Top each with the remaining dough circles.
12. With wet fingers, moisten the edges of each circle and press the edges to seal.
13. In the bottom of the prepared baking sheet, arrange the empanadas.
14. Cook in the oven for about 20 minutes.
15. Enjoy warm.

Western European Empanadas

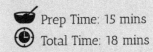 Prep Time: 15 mins

Total Time: 18 mins

Servings per Recipe: 30
Calories	95.1 kcal
Fat	5.7 g
Cholesterol	8.7 mg
Sodium	111.7 mg
Carbohydrates	7.5 g
Protein	3.5 g

Ingredients

Filling
1 tbsp. olive oil
1 tbsp. Spanish onion, chopped
3 garlic cloves, minced
1 tbsp. jalapeño, minced
1/4 C. red pepper , chopped
8 oz. picked lump crab meat
1 (4 oz.) packages goat cheese, or feta

1 tsp. chopped cilantro
1 tbsp. Italian parsley, chopped
7 oz. corn (drained)
1 tsp. cumin
salt
fresh ground black pepper
Pastry
2 sheets frozen pie dough, thawed

Directions

1. For the filling: in a skillet, add the oil over medium and cook until heated through.
2. Add the onion, red pepper, garlic and jalapeño and stir fry for about 5 minutes.
3. Remove from the heat and keep aside to cool completely.
4. In a bowl, add the remaining ingredients and mix until well combined.
5. Add the cooled onion mixture and mix well.
6. Place the dough onto a lightly floured surface and cut into 3-inch circles.
7. Place about 1/2-3/4 tbsp. of the filling in the center of each dough circle.
8. Fold the dough over the filling and press the edges to seal.
9. In the bottom of a tray, arrange the empanadas and place in the fridge for some time.
10. In a deep skillet, add 3-inch of the vegetable oil and cook until heated completely.
11. Add the empanadas in batches and cook until golden brown from both sides.
12. With a slotted spoon, transfer the empanadas onto a paper towel-lined plate to drain.
13. Enjoy warm.

CORN
Biscuit
Empanadas

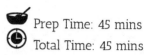 Prep Time: 45 mins
Total Time: 45 mins

Servings per Recipe: 1
Calories	445.8 kcal
Fat	23.1 g
Cholesterol	45.5 mg
Sodium	1221.8 mg
Carbohydrates	42.3 g
Protein	18.4 g

Ingredients

1 lb. ground beef
1 garlic clove
1 tsp. salt
1 (15 oz.) cans fresh cut corn, drained
1/2 C. chopped onion
8 oz. grated cheddar cheese
1 C. salsa

2 (16 oz.) cans large refrigerated biscuits

Directions

1. Set your oven to 375 degrees F before doing anything else and grease a baking sheet.
2. In a skillet, add the ground beef, salt and pepper and cook until cooked through.
3. Remove from the heat and keep aside to cool.
4. In a bowl, add the salsa, cheese, corn and onions and mix well.
5. Add the cooked beef and gently, stir to combine.
6. Place each biscuit onto a lightly floured surface and roll into an even thickness.
7. Place about 1/3 C. of the filling onto the center of each circle.
8. Fold the dough over the filling and press the edges to seal.
9. In the bottom of the prepared baking sheet, arrange the empanadas.
10. Cook in the oven until golden brown.
11. Enjoy warm.

Forest
Frost Empanadas

Prep Time: 10 mins
Total Time: 30 mins

Servings per Recipe: 12
Calories	238.7 kcal
Fat	13.1 g
Cholesterol	2.5 mg
Sodium	224.2 mg
Carbohydrates	28.5 g
Protein	2.4 g

Ingredients

1 lb. fresh blackberries
1 C. fresh apple, pared and finely chopped
1/4 C. chopped walnuts
1/4 C. sugar
2 tbsp. flour
1 tsp. ground cinnamon
1 tsp. vanilla

1 dash salt
3 (9 inch) pie crusts
1 tbsp. butter
Garnish
1/2 tsp. cinnamon
2 tbsp. sugar

Directions

1. Set your oven to 400 degrees F before doing anything else and grease a baking sheet.
2. In a bowl, add the walnuts, apple, and flour, sugar, cinnamon, salt and vanilla and mix until well combined.
3. Gently fold in the blackberries.
4. Place the pastry onto a lightly floured surface and unroll it.
5. Then, cut into 12 (4 1/2-inch) circles.
6. Place about 2 tbsp. of the filling onto half of each circle, leaving about 1/2-inch border.
7. Fold the dough over the filling and press the edges to seal.
8. In a bowl, add 2 tbsp. of the sugar and 1/2 tsp. of the cinnamon and mix well.
9. In the bottom of the prepared baking sheet, arrange the empanadas.
10. Coat each empanada with the melted butter and then, dust with the cinnamon sugar.
11. Cook in the oven for about 18-20 minutes.
12. Enjoy warm.

SWEET
Milk Empanadas

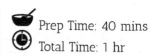
Servings per Recipe: 24
Calories	161.8 kcal
Fat	9.0 g
Cholesterol	44.8 mg
Sodium	26.0 mg
Carbohydrates	18.4 g
Protein	3.1 g

Ingredients

Dough
3 C. flour
3/4 C. cocoa powder, unsweetened
1/4-1/2 C. sugar
1 pinch salt
1 tsp. cinnamon
1 C. unsalted butter, cut into small pieces
2 eggs
4-6 tbsp. water
Filling

2 (16 oz.) jars dulce de leche, store bought, or see appendix
Optional
1 dash salt
1 egg, whisked with 1 tbsp. water to be used as egg wash
1/4 C. demerara sugar, to sprinkle on top of empanadas
Garnish
sprinkled with cocoa powder
1 scoop vanilla ice cream

Directions

1. For the dough: in a food processor, add the flour, cocoa powder, sugar, cinnamon and salt and pulse until well combined.
2. Add the butter pieces and pulse until well combined.
3. Add the eggs and water and pulse until a clumpy dough forms.
4. Transfer the dough onto a lightly floured surface and with your hands, knead for about 2 times.
5. Make 2 balls from the dough and with your hands, flatten each into a thick disc.
6. Place in the fridge for about 45-50 minutes.
7. Place the dough onto a lightly floured surface and roll into a thin circle.
8. With a round dough cutter, cut the circles from the dough.
9. Place the dulce de leche onto the center of each circle evenly.
10. Fold the dough over the filling and press the edges to seal.

11. In the bottom of a greased baking sheet, arrange the empanadas.
12. Coat the top of each empanada with the egg wash and dust with the demerara sugar lightly.
13. Place in for about 45 minutes.
14. Set your oven to 375 degrees F.
15. Cook in the oven for about 15-20 minutes.
16. Enjoy the empanadas warm with a dusting of the cocoa powder alongside the vanilla ice-cream.

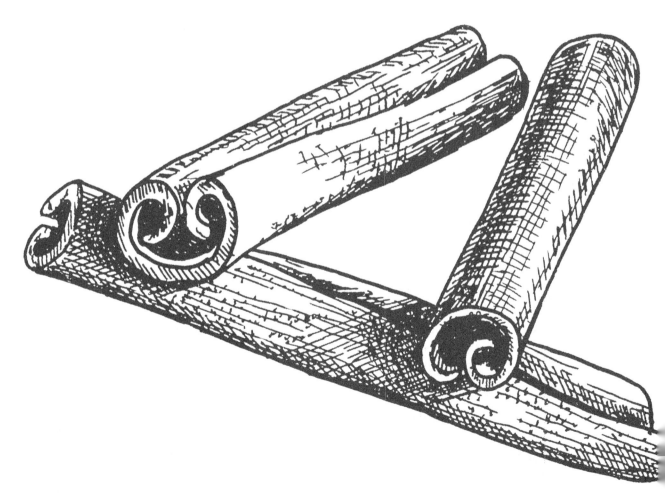

EAST
LA Empanada

🍳 Prep Time: 25 mins
🕐 Total Time: 55 mins

Servings per Recipe: 4
Calories	365.9 kcal
Fat	30.4 g
Cholesterol	139.2 mg
Sodium	200.5 mg
Carbohydrates	6.5 g
Protein	17.2 g

Ingredients

1 tbsp. olive oil
1/2 small onion, chopped
2 garlic cloves, minced
1/2 lb. ground beef
1/2 tsp. ground cumin
1/2 tsp. curry powder
1/2 tsp. chili powder
1/4 tsp. allspice
1/4 tsp. dried thyme

1 pinch kosher salt
1 pinch cinnamon
1 pinch ground pepper
1/2 C. frozen corn, defrosted
1/2 C. shredded white cheddar cheese
4 tbsp. unsalted butter
1 tbsp. sazon seasoning
12 empanada wrappers (6 inches)
1 egg, lightly beaten

Directions

1. In a skillet, add the oil over medium-high heat and cook until heated.
2. Add the onion and stir fry for about 3 minutes.
3. Add the garlic and stir fry for about 1 minute.
4. Stir in the beef, thyme, spices, salt and pepper and cook for about 10 minutes, mixing often.
5. Stir in the cheddar cheese and corn and remove from the heat.
6. Keep aside to cool completely.
7. Set your oven to 375 degrees F and line a baking sheet with the parchment paper.
8. In a frying pan add the butter and cook until melted.
9. Add the sazon powder and mix well.
10. Place about 2 heaping tbsp. of the filling onto the center of each wrapper.
11. Coat the edges of each wrapper with the beaten egg.
12. Fold the dough over the filling and press the edges to seal.
13. In the bottom of the prepared baking sheet, arrange the empanadas and coat the top of

each with the melted butter.
14. Cook in the oven for about 20 minutes.
15. Enjoy warm.

EMPANADAS
in October

Prep Time: 30 mins
Total Time: 50 mins

Servings per Recipe: 1

Calories	76.8 kcal
Fat	4.1 g
Cholesterol	13.5 mg
Sodium	82.8 mg
Carbohydrates	9.3 g
Protein	0.8 g

Ingredients

Filling
1 C. canned pumpkin
1 C. brown sugar
1 tbsp. butter
1 tsp. ground cinnamon
1 tsp. pumpkin pie spice
1/4 C. chopped pecans
Crust
2 1/2 C. all-purpose flour

2 tbsp. granulated sugar
1 tsp. salt
1 C. cold butter
8-10 tbsp. cold water
Glaze
1 egg
1 tsp. water
Garnish
sanding sugar

Directions

1. In a pot, add the pumpkin, 1 tbsp. of the butter, brown sugar, pumpkin pie spice and cinnamon over medium heat and cook for about 10-12 minutes, mixing continuously.
2. Remove from the heat and keep aside to cool completely.
3. After cooling, add the pecans and stir to combine.
4. Set your oven to 400 degrees F.
5. In a bowl, add the flour, salt and sugar and mix well.
6. With a pastry blender, cut in 1 C. of the butter until a coarse crumb like mixture is formed.
7. Add enough water and mix until just combined.
8. Place the dough onto a lightly floured surface and cut into 2 equal sized pieces.
9. Now, roll each piece into 1/8-inch thickness.
10. With a 2 1/2-inch round cookie cutter, cut the circles from each dough piece.
11. Place about rounded 1/2 tsp. of the filling onto the center of each dough circle.
12. Fold the dough over the filling and press the edges to seal.
13. In a bowl, add egg and 1 tsp. of the water and beat well.

14. In the bottom of a ungreased baking sheet, arrange the empanadas.
15. Coat top of each empanada with the egg wash and dust with the adding sugar.
16. Cook in the oven for about 12-15 minutes.
17. Enjoy warm.

FATHIA'S
Favorite
Empanadas

Prep Time: 0 mins
Total Time: 15 mins

Servings per Recipe: 16	
Calories	181.9 kcal
Fat	11.8 g
Cholesterol	44.7 mg
Sodium	869.6 mg
Carbohydrates	9.0 g
Protein	11.0 g

Ingredients

1/2 lb. white-meat ground turkey
1/2 tsp. salt
1/4 tsp. pepper
1/4 tsp. cumin
1/4 tsp. sweet chili powder
1 tbsp. olive oil
1 (15 oz.) cans diced tomatoes, drained

1 C. olive, chopped
2 tbsp. chopped pickled jalapeño peppers
vegetable oil cooking spray
1 lb. raw frozen pizza dough

Directions

1. Set your oven to 400 degrees F before doing anything else and grease a baking sheet.
2. In a bowl, mix together the cumin, chili, powder, salt and pepper.
3. Season the turkey with the spice mixture evenly.
4. In a skillet, add the oil over high heat and cook until heated.
5. Add the turkey and cook for about 3-4 minutes, breaking up the meat.
6. Add the olives, tomatoes and jalapeños and stir to combine.
7. Set the heat to low and cook, covered for about 3-4 minutes.
8. Place the dough onto a lightly floured surface and cut into 4 equal sized pieces.
9. Now, stretch each dough piece into 8-inch circle.
10. Place about 1/2 C. of the turkey mixture onto each dough circle.
11. Fold the dough over the filling and press the edges to seal.
12. In the bottom of the prepared baking sheet, arrange the empanadas and spray each with cooking spray.
13. Cook in the oven for about 10-15 minutes.
14. Enjoy warm.

Cannellin
Chicken Empanadas

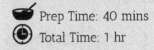 Prep Time: 40 mins

Total Time: 1 hr

Servings per Recipe: 20
Calories	108.7 kcal
Fat	6.0 g
Cholesterol	24.7 mg
Sodium	190.0 mg
Carbohydrates	5.8 g
Protein	7.7 g

Ingredients

1 lb. chicken legs with thigh
2 tbsp. olive oil
1 (1/2 oz.) packet sazon goya
1 tbsp. oregano
1 tsp. salt
1 C. cheddar cheese, shredded
15 1/2 oz. cannellini beans, drained

1/4 C. salsa
20 empanada wrappers (goya discos)

Directions

1. In a skillet, add the oil and cook until heated.
2. Add the chicken and cook until browned completely.
3. Add the oregano, sazon and enough water to cover the chicken in half and cook for about 30-40 minutes.
4. Drain the chicken completely and keep aside to cool slightly.
5. Remove the skin of chicken legs and then, shred the meat.
6. In a bowl, add the shredded chicken, cheddar cheese, cannellini beans and salsa and mix well.
7. Keep aside to cool completely.
8. Set your oven to 375 degrees F.
9. Place about 1-2 tbsp. of the chicken mixture onto the center of each disco.
10. Fold the dough over the filling and press the edges to seal.
11. In the bottom of a baking sheet, arrange the empanadas and coat the top of each with the butter.
12. Cook in the oven for about 15-20 minutes.
13. Enjoy warm.

EMPANADAS
in College

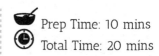

Prep Time: 10 mins
Total Time: 20 mins

Servings per Recipe: 4
Calories   370.5 kcal
Fat   13.7 g
Cholesterol   70.3 mg
Sodium   947.2 mg
Carbohydrates   32.1 g
Protein   28.7 g

Ingredients

1 lb. extra lean ground beef
8 refrigerated biscuits, such as Pillsbury
Grands
1 (1 1/4 oz.) envelopes taco seasoning
1/4 C. water
1 (14 1/2 oz.) cans petite diced
tomatoes

1 C. store bought salsa con queso sauce,
such as Pace

Directions

1. Set your oven to 450 degrees F before doing anything else.
2. In a nonstick skillet, add the beef over high heat and cook until meat is no more pink, breaking up the meat.
3. Meanwhile, place each biscuit onto a lightly floured surface and roll into a 4 1/2-inch (1/2-inch thick) circle.
4. In the bottom of an ungreased baking sheet, arrange the flattened biscuits.
5. Add the taco seasoning mix and water into the beef and stir to combine.
6. Remove from the heat.
7. Place about 2 tbsp. of the beef mixture onto the center of each biscuit.
8. Fold the dough over the filling and press the edges to seal.
9. Cook in the oven for about 8 minutes.
10. Meanwhile, in the same skillet with leftover beef mixture, add the salsa sauce and tomatoes with juice over low heat and cook until heated completely, mixing occasionally.
11. Enjoy the warm empanadas with a topping of the cheese sauce.

Baja
Empanadas

🍲 Prep Time: 1 hr
🕐 Total Time: 2 hrs 30 mins

Servings per Recipe: 6	
Calories	515.8 kcal
Fat	34.3 g
Cholesterol	83.0 mg
Sodium	897.3 mg
Carbohydrates	40.0 g
Protein	12.7 g

Ingredients

Dough
2 C. all-purpose flour
1/2 C. lard, chilled
2 1/2 tbsp. unsalted butter, chilled
1/2 tsp. salt
about 1/3 C. ice water
Filling
2 tbsp. olive oil
1 large white onion, diced
1/2 tsp. salt

1/2 tsp. fresh ground black pepper
2 bunches Swiss chard, about 1 lb. total weight, trimmed, leaves cut into small pieces and stems cut into 1/2 inch dice
3/4 C. Cotija cheese
1/4 C. asadero cheese, grated, or cheddar
fresh lime juice
1 egg, beaten, for the glaze
freshly cracked pepper

Directions

1. For the Dough: in a bowl, add the flour, salt, butter and lard and with your fingers, mix until coarse crumb like mixture forms.
2. Slowly, add the ice water, a little at a time and with a fork, mix until a dough forms.
3. With your hands, knead until a dough ball is formed.
4. With a plastic wrap, cover the dough an place in the fridge overnight.
5. For the filling: in a skillet, add the oil over medium heat and cook until heated.
6. Add the onion, salt and pepper and stir fry for about 8-10 minutes.
7. Add the chard stems and cook for about 1-2 minutes.
8. Add the chard leaves and stir fry for about 3-4 minutes.
9. Transfer the chard mixture into a bowl and keep aside to cool.
10. Add the lime juice and cheeses and stir to combine.
11. Place each biscuit onto a lightly floured surface and roll into a 1/8-inch thickness.
12. With a 3-inch round cookie cutter, cut 12 equal sized circles from the dough.

13. Place about 2 tsp. of the filling onto one half of each circle, leaving about 1/2-inch edge.
14. Coat the edges of each circle with the beaten egg.
15. Fold the dough over the filling and press the edges to seal.
16. In the bottom of a tray, place the empanadas in a single layer.
17. With a plastic wrap, cover the tray and place in the fridge for about 2 hours.
18. Set your oven to 350 degrees F and grease a baking sheet.
19. In the bottom of the prepared baking sheet, arrange the empanadas.
20. Coat the edges of each circle with the beaten egg and dust with the cracked pepper.
21. Cook in the oven for about 30 minutes.
22. Enjoy warm

Jalapeno
Party Empanada

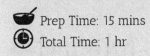 Prep Time: 15 mins

Total Time: 1 hr

Servings per Recipe: 6

Calories	684.4 kcal
Fat	43.0 g
Cholesterol	93.8 mg
Sodium	562.9 mg
Carbohydrates	44.1 g
Protein	30.5 g

Ingredients

1 1/2 lb. ground sirloin
1 onion, chopped
2 jalapeños, chopped
2 Roma tomatoes, chopped
1/2 C. rice, cooked
1/2 C. Monterey jack cheese, shredded
1 tbsp. chili powder
1 tbsp. garlic powder
salt
pepper

2 refrigerated pie crusts
Garnish
4 tbsp. green onions, chopped
1/4 C. shredded Monterey Jack cheese
1/2 C. cilantro, chopped
1 Roma tomato, chopped
1 C. romaine lettuce, chopped
1/2 C. salsa
6 tbsp. sour cream
1 avocado, sliced

Directions

1. Set your oven to 400 degrees F before doing anything else and line a baking sheet with the parchment paper.
2. In a skillet, add the ground sirloin, rice, onion, tomato and jalapeños and cook until meat is browned completely.
3. Stir in 1/2 C. of the cheese and spices and remove from the heat.
4. In the bottom of the prepared baking sheet, place 1 pie crust and unroll it.
5. Place the meat mixture onto the center of crust, leaving about 1 1/2-inch border.
6. Roll the second crust and arrange on top of the meat mixture.
7. With a fork, press the edges to seal.
8. With a fork, poke several holes on top of the crust.
9. Cook in the oven for about 40 minutes.
10. Cut into 6 wedges and enjoy warm alongside all topping ingredients.

WEDNESDAY'S
25-Minute Empanadas

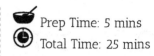 Prep Time: 5 mins
Total Time: 25 mins

Servings per Recipe: 8
Calories   619.7 kcal
Fat   39.7 g
Cholesterol   37.2 mg
Sodium   1078.8 mg
Carbohydrates   54.6 g
Protein   10.3 g

Ingredients

1 (3 oz.) packets solid white tuna, drained and flaked
1 (4 oz.) cans diced green chilies, drained
1 (2 1/2 oz.) cans of sliced black olives, drained
1/2 C. of shredded sharp cheddar cheese
1 hard-boiled egg, chopped
salt and pepper
1/4 tsp. hot pepper sauce
1/4 C. of medium thick chunky salsa
2 (15 oz.) packages refrigerated pie crusts
additional salsa

Directions

1. Set your oven to 425 degrees F before doing anything else and line a baking sheet with a piece of the foil.
2. In a bowl, add the tuna, egg, cheese, olives, chilies, hot sauce, salt and pepper and toss to coat well.
3. Add 1/4 C. of the salsa and toss to coat.
4. Prepare the pie crust as suggested on the package.
5. Unfold the pie crusts and cut each into 4 (4-inch) circles.
6. In the bottom of the prepared baking sheet, arrange 8 dough circles.
7. Place about 1/4 C. of the tuna mixture onto the center of each dough circle.
8. With wet fingers, moisten the edges of each circle.
9. Cover each with the remaining dough circles and press edges together to seal.
10. With a knife, cut slits in top of each empanada.
11. Cook in the oven for about 15-18 minutes.
12. Enjoy warm alongside the extra salsa.

Holiday
Empanadas

Prep Time: 30 mins
Total Time: 45 mins

Servings per Recipe: 6
Calories	459.2 kcal
Fat	21.6 g
Cholesterol	107.5 mg
Sodium	404.5 mg
Carbohydrates	31.6 g
Protein	32.9 g

Ingredients

1 1 sheet frozen puff pastry
2 C. mashed potatoes
4 C. cooked turkey, shredded
1 tbsp. chili powder
1/4 C. fresh parsley, chopped
1/4 C. fresh cilantro, chopped
salt & freshly ground black pepper

1 egg, beaten with
1 tbsp. water
all-purpose flour, for dusting

Directions

1. Remove one puff pastry sheet from the freezer and place in the fridge for about 30 minutes.
2. Set your oven to 400 degrees F and line a baking sheet with the parchment paper.
3. Meanwhile, for the filling: in a bowl, add the turkey, mashed potatoes, cilantro, parsley, chili powder, salt and black pepper and mix well.
4. Place the dough onto a lightly floured surface and roll into 1/8-inch thickness.
5. Cut the rolled dough in half horizontally and then, cut each into 3 equal sized squares.
6. Place about 1/3 C. of the turkey mixture onto the center of each square.
7. Fold the dough over the filling to make a triangle and press the edges to seal.
8. In the bottom of the prepared baking sheet, arrange the empanadas and coat each with the egg wash.
9. Cook in the oven for about 10-15 minutes.
10. Enjoy hot.

HOLIDAY
Empanadas

 Prep Time: 30 mins

Total Time: 45 mins

Servings per Recipe: 6
Calories	459.2 kcal
Fat	21.6 g
Cholesterol	107.5 mg
Sodium	404.5 mg
Carbohydrates	31.6 g
Protein	32.9 g

Ingredients

1 sheet frozen puff pastry
2 C. mashed potatoes
4 C. cooked turkey, shredded
1 tbsp. chili powder
1/4 C. fresh parsley, chopped
1/4 C. fresh cilantro, chopped
salt & freshly ground black pepper

1 egg, beaten with
1 tbsp. water
all-purpose flour, for dusting

Directions

1. Remove one puff pastry sheet from the freezer and place in the fridge for about 30 minutes.
2. Set your oven to 400 degrees F and line a baking sheet with the parchment paper.
3. Meanwhile, for the filling: in a bowl, add the turkey, mashed potatoes, cilantro, parsley, chili powder, salt and black pepper and mix well.
4. Place the dough onto a lightly floured surface and roll into 1/8-inch thickness.
5. Cut the rolled dough in half horizontally and then, cut each into 3 equal sized squares.
6. Place about 1/3 C. of the turkey mixture onto the center of each square.
7. Fold the dough over the filling to make a triangle and press the edges to seal.
8. In the bottom of the prepared baking sheet, arrange the empanadas and coat each with the egg wash.
9. Cook in the oven for about 10-15 minutes.
10. Enjoy hot.

Empanadas
Caribana

Prep Time: 45 mins
Total Time: 55 mins

Servings per Recipe: 6
Calories	316.3 kcal
Fat	2.0 g
Cholesterol	35.2 mg
Sodium	413.1 mg
Carbohydrates	70.9 g
Protein	5.7 g

Ingredients

Dough
1 tsp. oil
1/4 C. sugar
1 tsp. salt
2 C. flour
3/4 C. water
Filling

8 oz. guava jelly
1/2 C. sliced mango
1 tbsp. mint, minced
1 lemon, juiced
1 egg, lightly beaten

Directions

1. In the bowl of a stand mixer with the paddle attachment, add the flour, salt and sugar and mix well.
2. Add the water and oil and mix until a dough forms.
3. Place the dough onto a floured surface and roll into 1/8-inch thickness.
4. With a 3-inch round cutter, cut the circles from the dough.
5. In a bowl, add the mango, guava jelly, mint and lemon juice and mix until well combined.
6. Place the guava filling onto the center of each dough circle.
7. Coat the edges with the egg wash.
8. Fold the dough over the filling and press the edges to seal.
9. In a deep skillet, add the oil and cook until its temperature reaches to 375 degrees F.
10. Add the empanadas in batches and cook until golden brown.
11. With a slotted spoon, transfer the empanadas onto a paper towels-lined plate to drain.
12. Enjoy warm.

NEW MEXICAN
Empanadas

Prep Time: 1 hr mins

Total Time: 1 hr 30 mins

Servings per Recipe: 4

Calories	771.0 kcal
Fat	44.0 g
Cholesterol	346.8 mg
Sodium	3437.0 mg
Carbohydrates	59.1 g
Protein	35.1 g

Ingredients

11 lb. ground chicken
1 jalapeño, diced
1/2 medium onion, diced
1 garlic clove, minced
1 tbsp. cumin
1 tsp. chili powder
1 tsp. paprika
1/2 tsp. salt
1/2 tsp. cayenne pepper
1/2 C. Mexican cheese (cotija)
1 tsp. olive oil

Dough
3 egg yolks
2 1/4 C. flour
1/2 C. butter
1 1/2 tsp. salt
1 large egg
1/3 C. ice water
1 tbsp. of distilled white vinegar
Spice
1 tbsp. salt
1 tbsp. chili powderl

Directions

1. For the dough: in a bowl, sift together the flour and salt.
2. With a pastry blender, cut in the butter until a crumbly mixture forms.
3. In another bowl, add the egg, water and vinegar and whisk until foamy.
4. Add the egg mixture into the flour mixture and with a fork, mix until well combined.
5. Now, with your hands, knead the dough for some time.
6. Place the dough onto a floured surface and roll into a triangle.
7. With a plastic wrap, cover the dough and refrigerate for about 1 hour.
8. For the chicken: in a pan, add 1 tsp. of the oil over medium heat and cook until heated.
9. Add the onion, garlic and jalapeño, and stir fry for about 3-4 minutes.
10. Stir in the ground chicken, cumin, cayenne pepper, paprika, chili powder and salt and cook until meat is no more pink, breaking up the meat.
11. Drain the grease well and transfer the chicken mixture into a bowl.

12. Keep aside for about 5 minutes.
13. Add the Mexican cheese into the bowl of the chicken mixture and mix well.
14. Keep aside for about 10 minutes.
15. Set your oven to 400 degrees F before doing anything else and grease a baking sheet.
16. Place the dough onto a floured surface and rolled into 1/2-inch thickness.
17. Then, cut 4 inch circles from the dough.
18. Place about 2 tbsp. of the chicken mixture onto the center of each circle.
19. Fold the dough over the filling and press the edges to seal.
20. In a bowl, mix together the chili powder and salt.
21. In the bottom of the prepared baking sheet, arrange the empanadas.
22. Coat each empanada with the egg yolk and sprinkle with the salt mixture.
23. Cook in the oven for about 12-14 minutes.
24. Enjoy warm.

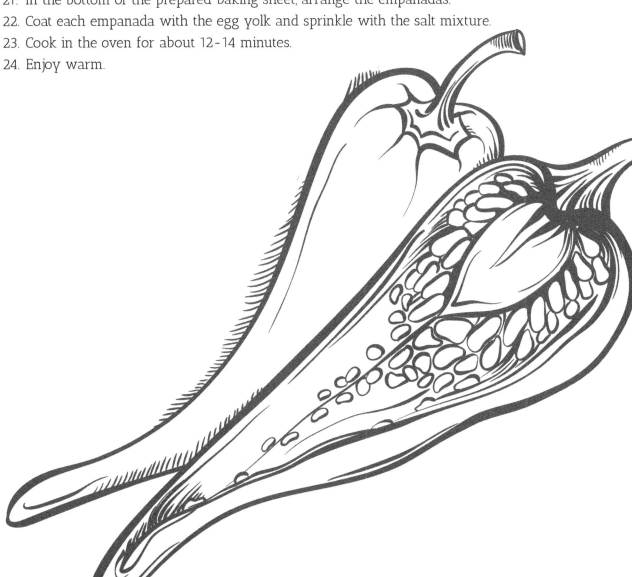

SWEET
Bean Empanadas

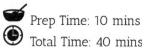 Prep Time: 10 mins
Total Time: 40 mins

Servings per Recipe: 1
Calories	333.9 kcal
Fat	21.3 g
Cholesterol	23.8 mg
Sodium	159.4 mg
Carbohydrates	27.9 g
Protein	8.3 g

Ingredients

2 tbsp. vegetable oil
1 firm medium-size banana, diced
3/4 C. chopped onion
1 (15 oz.) cans black beans, drained
1/4 C. chopped fresh cilantro
3/4 tsp. ground cumin
1/4 tsp. cayenne pepper

1 (17 1/3 oz.) packages frozen puff pastry, thawed, 2 sheets
1 C. grated Monterey Jack cheese
1 egg, beaten to blend

Directions

1. In a skillet, add the oil over high heat and cook until heated through.
2. Add the banana pieces and stir fry for about 1 1/2 minutes.
3. With a slotted spoon, transfer the banana pieces onto the paper towels-lined plate to drain.
4. In the same skillet, add the onion and stir fry for about 3 minutes.
5. Stir in the beans, cilantro, cayenne and cumin and cook for about 3 minutes.
6. Stir in the salt and remove from the heat.
7. With the back of a fork, mash the beans mixture until a coarse paste is formed.
8. Keep aside to cool completely.
9. Set your oven to 425 degrees F.
10. Place each puff pastry onto a lightly floured surface and roll into 9-inch squares.
11. Then, cut each square into 9 squares.
12. Place 1 heaping tbsp. of the beans mixture onto the center of 12 squares, followed by the cheese and banana pieces evenly.
13. Coat the edges of each square with the beaten egg.
14. Fold the dough over the filling to form a triangle and press the edges to seal.
15. In the bottom of a rimmed baking sheet, arrange the empanadas.

16. Cook in the oven for about 15 minutes.
17. Enjoy warm.

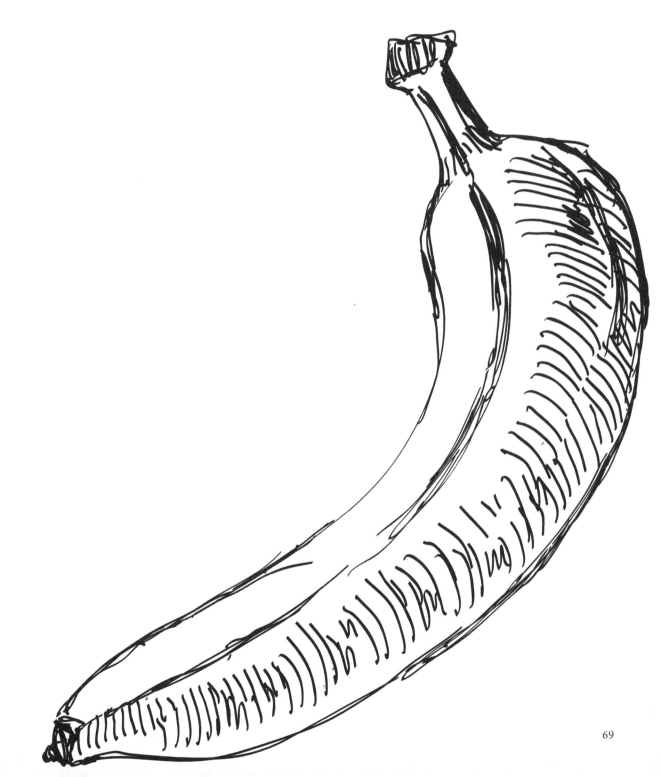

FLAVORS
of November
Empanadas

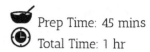

Prep Time: 45 mins
Total Time: 1 hr

Servings per Recipe: 1
Calories	370.5 kcal
Fat	13.7 g
Cholesterol	70.3 mg
Sodium	947.2 mg
Carbohydrates	32.1 g
Protein	28.7 g

Ingredients

Crust
3 C. all-purpose flour
1 1/2 tbsp. sugar
1/2 tsp. salt
9 tbsp. well chilled shortening
2/3-1 C. milk
Filling
1 tbsp. shortening

1 C. chopped onion
1 tbsp. brown sugar
1 tsp. fresh thyme leaves or 1/4 tsp. dried thyme leaves
3/4 tsp. salt
1 (15 oz.) cans pumpkin puree
1/2 C. ricotta cheese
2/3 C. graded Parmesan cheese

Directions

1. For the dough: in a food processor, add the flour, salt, sugar and shortening and process until a coarse crumb like mixture is formed.
2. While the motor is running, slowly add the milk, 1 tbsp. at a time until dough forms.
3. Place the dough onto a lightly floured surface and divide into 3 round disks.
4. With a plastic wrap, cover the dough and refrigerate for about 1 hour.
5. For the filling: in a skillet, add the shortening over medium heat and cook until heated through.
6. Add the onion and cook for about 5-6 minutes.
7. Add the thyme, brown sugar and salt and stir to combine.
8. Stir in the pumpkin, Parmesan and ricotta, and remove from the heat.
9. Place the dough onto a lightly floured surface and cut into 12 equal sized pieces.
10. Now, roll each piece into a 6-inch circle.
11. Place about 1/4 C. of the pumpkin mixture onto each circle.
12. With wet fingers, moisten the edges of each circle.
13. Fold the dough over the filling and press the edges to seal.

14. In a deep skillet, add 1-inch deep oil over medium heat and cook until its temperature reaches to 350 degrees F.
15. Add the empanadas in batches and cook for about 2-2 1/2 minutes per side.
16. With a slotted spoon, transfer the empanadas onto a paper towels-lined plate to drain.
17. Enjoy warm.

NEW ENGLAND
House Empanadas

 Prep Time: 20 mins

Total Time: 38 mins

Servings per Recipe: 16

Calories	215.9 kcal
Fat	15.2 g
Cholesterol	5.5 mg
Sodium	245.2 mg
Carbohydrates	15.2 g
Protein	4.7 g

Ingredients

2 sheets frozen puff pastry, thawed
flour, for dusting
1 C. shredded fresh Parmesan cheese
cooking spray
2 tbsp. Hidden Valley Original Ranch
Seasoning Mix
2 tbsp. olive oil

1 C. onion, thinly sliced
2 garlic cloves, minced
1 C. cleaned shrimp, chopped
1 C. chopped turkey bacon, cooked
1/2 tsp. salt
1/2 tsp. smoked paprika
1/4 tsp. black pepper

Directions

1. Set your oven to 325 degrees F before doing anything else and arrange the racks in upper and lower thirds of the oven.
2. Line 2 baking sheets with the parchment papers.
3. In a bowl, add the Parmesan and spray with cooking oil lightly.
4. Add the Ranch seasoning mix and toss to coat well.
5. In a skillet, add the oil and cook until heated through.
6. Add the onions and cook for about 9-10 minutes.
7. Add the garlic and cook for about 1-2 minutes.
8. Add the shrimp, paprika, salt and pepper and stir to combine.
9. Add the bacon and chives and toss to coat.
10. Remove from the heat and keep aside.
11. Place each puff pastry sheet onto a floured surface and roll into 1/8-inch thickness.
12. With a cookie cutter, cut 8 circles from each pastry sheet.
13. Place about 2 tbsp. of the filling onto the center of each dough circle, followed by the seasoned cheese.
14. With wet fingers, moisten the edges of each circle.

15. Fold the dough over the filling and press the edges to seal.
16. In the bottom of the prepared baking sheet, arrange the empanadas and coat each with the egg wash.
17. Cook in the oven for about 18-20 minutes, rotating the baking sheets once half way through.
18. Enjoy warm.

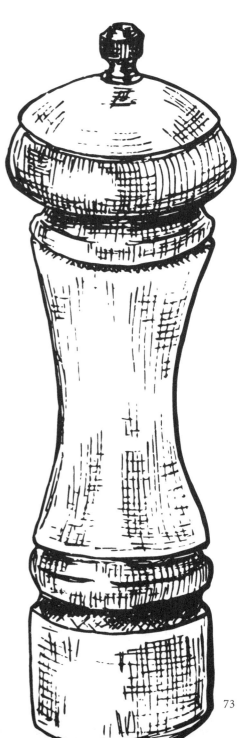

CREAM
Cheese
Empanadas

Prep Time: 3 hrs
Total Time: 3 hrs 40 mins

Servings per Recipe: 1
Calories	241.0 kcal
Fat	14.6 g
Cholesterol	48.2 mg
Sodium	253.6 mg
Carbohydrates	25.8 g
Protein	2.5 g

Ingredients

1 1 C. butter, chilled and chopped
8 oz. cream cheese, chilled and chopped
2 1/3 C. flour
1 tbsp. sugar
1 tsp. salt
1 tsp. vanilla
Filling
2 tbsp. butter
4-5 firm green apples, peeled, cored

and cubed
1/2 C. sugar
1-2 tsp. cinnamon
1/4 C. brown sugar
2 tbsp. cornstarch
1 pinch salt
3 tbsp. dulce de leche
1 egg yolk
sugar, for sprinkling

Directions

1. For the dough: in a food processor, add the flour, sugar and salt and process slightly.
2. Add the cream cheese and butter and process until just mixture starts to come together.
3. Add the vanilla and process 2 times.
4. Place the dough onto a plastic wrap piece and with your hands, shape into a disk.
5. With a plastic wrap, cover the dough and refrigerate overnight.
6. For the filling: in a pan, add the butter, apples, sugars, cinnamon and salt over medium heat and cook until apples are just tender.
7. In a bowl, add the cornstarch and 1-2 tbsp. of the water and beat until smooth.
8. Add the cornstarch mixture into the apples mixture and cook until mixture starts too thick, stirring continuously.
9. Remove from the heat and stir in the dulce de leche.
10. Transfer the mixture into a bowl and place in the fridge for about 2 hours, mixing often.
11. Place the dough onto a lightly floured surface and roll into 1/4-1/8-inch thickness.
12. Now, cut the dough into 6-inch circles.

13. Place about 1 scant tbsp. of the filling onto the center of each dough circle.
14. With wet fingers, moisten the edges of each circle.
15. Fold the dough over the filling and press the edges to seal.
16. In the bottom of a baking sheet, arrange the empanadas and refrigerate for about 1 hour.
17. Set your oven to 350 degrees F.
18. In a bowl, add the egg yolk and a little water and beat well.
19. Coat each empanada with the egg wash and dust with the sugar.
20. Cook in the oven for about 20 minutes.
21. Enjoy warm.

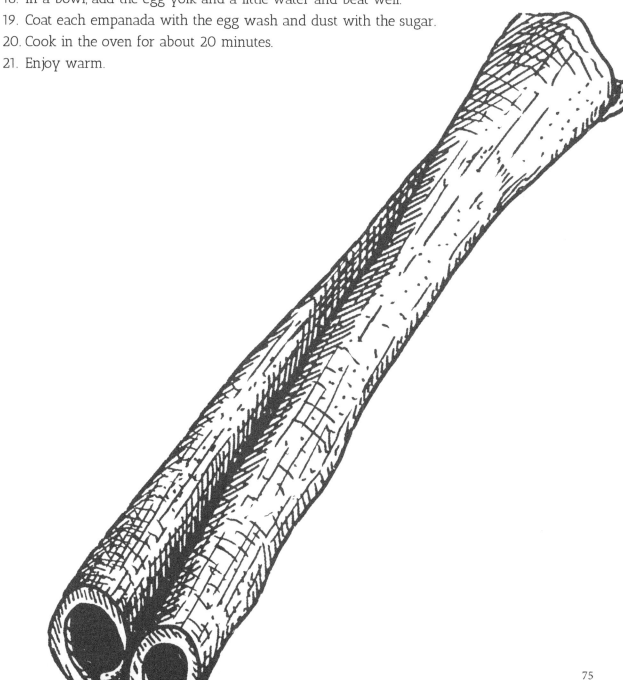

SWEET
Caramel Empanadas

 Prep Time: 15 mins

Total Time: 30 mins

Servings per Recipe: 36	
Calories	202.7 kcal
Fat	2.7 g
Cholesterol	0.2 mg
Sodium	338.2 mg
Carbohydrates	38.5 g
Protein	6.0 g

Ingredients

1 (36 count) packages frozen rolls,
dough thawed per package directions
10 caramel candies, each 4 pieces
1/3 C. all-purpose flour
3 C. apples, peeled and chopped
2/3 C. caramel ice cream topping
2 tsp. lemon juice

Directions

1. Set your oven to 375 degrees F before doing anything else and lightly, grease 2 baking sheets.
2. In a bowl, add the flour and caramel pieces and mix well.
3. Add the caramel topping, apples and lemon juice and mix until well combined.
4. Place each dough roll onto a lightly floured surface and roll into a 4-inch circle.
5. Place about 2 tbsp. of the apple mixture onto the lower half of each dough circle.
6. Coat the edges with the milk.
7. Fold the dough over the filling and press the edges to seal.
8. In the bottom of the prepared baking sheets, arrange the empanadas.
9. Cook in the oven for about 15 minutes.
10. Enjoy warm.

Hot
Empanadas

Prep Time: 20 mins
Total Time: 40 mins

Servings per Recipe: 4
Calories	813.4 kcal
Fat	51.4 g
Cholesterol	92.0 mg
Sodium	1166.0 mg
Carbohydrates	53.6 g
Protein	32.5 g

Ingredients

3/4 lb. lean ground beef
1/3 C. chopped green onion
1/3 C. buffalo wing sauce
1 (16 1/3 oz.) cans grands refrigerator biscuits
1 C. shredded Monterey Jack cheese
1/2 C. ranch salad dressing, optional for

dipping

Directions

1. Set your oven to 375 degrees F before doing anything else.
2. In a skillet, add the ground beef over medium-high heat and cook for about 5-7 minutes, breaking up the meat.
3. Drain the grease from the skillet.
4. Stir in the onions and buffalo sauce and remove from the heat.
5. Separate the dough into 8 biscuits.
6. Place each biscuit onto a lightly floured surface and roll into a 6-inch circle.
7. Place the beef mixture onto half of each biscuit and top each with 2 tbsp. of the cheese.
8. Fold the dough over the filling and press the edges to seal.
9. In the bottom of an ungreased baking sheet, arrange the empanadas.
10. Cook in the oven for about 12-17 minutes.
11. Enjoy warm alongside the ranch dressing

CLASSICAL
Empanadas

Prep Time: 2 hrs
Total Time: 2 hrs 20 mins

Servings per Recipe: 24
Calories	370.5 kcal
Fat	13.7 g
Cholesterol	70.3 mg
Sodium	947.2 mg
Carbohydrates	32.1 g
Protein	28.7 g

Ingredients

Dough
3 3/4 C. unbleached all-purpose flour,
plus more for dusting the work surface
1 tbsp. sugar
1 1/2 tsp. salt
12 tbsp. unsalted butter, 1/2-inch cubes
and frozen for 10 minutes
1 1/4 C. ice water
1 large egg, beaten
Filling
1 tbsp. olive oil
1 medium onion, minced

1 tbsp. tomato paste
2 medium garlic cloves, minced
1 tsp. minced fresh oregano leaves
1 tsp. ground cumin
1 pinch ground cloves
1 pinch cayenne pepper
1/2 lb. ground chuck
3/4 C. low-sodium beef broth
1 tsp. sugar
salt and ground black pepper
2 oz. monterey jack cheese, shredded

Directions

1. For the dough: in a food processor, add the flour, salt and sugar and pulse until just combined.
2. Add the butter pieces and pulse until a coarse crumb like mixture is formed.
3. Transfer the flour mixture into a bowl.
4. Slowly, add the water, 1/4 C. at a time and with a rubber spatula, mix until a dough forms.
5. Place the dough onto a lightly floured surface and cut into 2 equal sized portions.
6. With your hands, flatten each dough portion into a 6-inch disk.
7. With a plastic wrap, wrap each dough disk and place in the fridge for about 3 hours.
8. Line 2 baking sheets with parchment paper; set aside.
9. Place each dough disk onto a lightly floured surface and roll each into an 18-inch circle.
10. With a 3-inch cookie cutter, cut circles from the dough.

11. In the bottom of 2 parchment paper lined baking sheets, arrange the dough circles.
12. With a plastic wrap, cover each baking sheet and place in the fridge until using.
13. For the filling: in a nonstick skillet, add the oil over medium-high heat and cook until heated.
14. Add the onion and stir fry for about 5-7 minutes.
15. Stir in the garlic, tomato paste, oregano, cloves, cumin and cayenne and stir fry for about 40 seconds.
16. Stir in the beef and cook for about 4-5 minutes, breaking up the meat.
17. Add the broth and stir to combine well.
18. Reduce the heat to low and cook for about 7-8 minutes.
19. Stir in the sugar, salt and pepper and remove from the heat.
20. Place the beef mixture into a bowl.
21. With a plastic wrap, cover the bowl and place in the fridge for about 1 hour.
22. Now, stir in the cheese and place in the fridge until using.
23. Set your oven to 425 degrees F and arrange a rack in the lower-middle position of the rack.
24. Line 2 baking sheets with the parchment paper.
25. Place about 1 tsp. of the filling onto the center of each dough circle.
26. With wet fingers, moisten the edges of each circle.
27. Fold the dough over the filling and press the edges to seal.
28. In the bottom of the prepared baking sheets, arrange the empanadas and coat each with the beaten egg.
29. Cook in the oven for about 20 minutes, rotating the baking sheets once halfway through.
30. Enjoy warm.

SIMPLE
South American Empanadas

Prep Time: 10 mins
Total Time: 15 mins

Servings per Recipe: 6
Calories   902.5 kcal
Fat   78.3 g
Cholesterol   4.8 mg
Sodium   256.0 mg
Carbohydrates   45.2 g
Protein   5.9 g

Ingredients

12 oz. all-purpose flour
1 tsp. baking powder
1 oz. shortening
1/2 tsp. salt
3/4 C. warm water
1/2 tsp. lemon juice
1/2 lb. white cheese, shredded

2 tsp. sugar
2 C. oil, for frying

Directions

1. In a bowl, add the flour and baking powder and mix well.
2. With a pastry blender, cut in the shortening until a coarse crumb like mixture forms.
3. In another bowl, add the water, lemon juice and salt and mix well.
4. Slowly, add the salt mixture into the flour mixture and mix until a soft dough forms.
5. Now, with your hands, knead the dough well.
6. Place the dough onto a lightly floured surface and roll into a thin circle.
7. With a round cookie cutter, cut circles from the dough.
8. Place about 1 tbsp. of the cheese onto each dough circle.
9. Fold the dough over the filling and press the edges to seal.
10. In a deep skillet, add the oil and cook until heated through.
11. Add the empanadas in batches and cook until golden brown.
12. With a slotted spoon, transfer the empanadas onto a paper towels-lined plate to drain.
13. Enjoy warm with a dusting of the sugar.

How
to Make Empanada Crust

🥣 Prep Time: 1 hr 30 mins
🕐 Total Time: 1 hr 50 mins

Servings per Recipe: 1
Calories	134.6 kcal
Fat	3.7 g
Cholesterol	37.7 mg
Sodium	234.6 mg
Carbohydrates	21.7 g
Protein	3.0 g

Ingredients

2 C. flour
1 tsp. salt
2 tbsp. sugar
2 tbsp. cooking oil
2 egg yolks
1/4 C. water
cornstarch, to prevent dough from sticking

oil

Directions

1. In a bowl, add the flour, sugar and salt and mix well.
2. Now, sift the flour mixture into a second bowl.
3. In another bowl, add the egg yolks, oil and water and beat until well combined.
4. Add the flour mixture and mix until well combined.
5. With your hand, knead until a smooth dough forms.
6. With a plastic wrap, cover the dough and refrigerate for about 1 hour before using.

CHOPPED
Burger
Empanadas

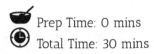
Prep Time: 0 mins
Total Time: 30 mins

Servings per Recipe: 4
Calories	456.0 kcal
Fat	29.9 g
Cholesterol	27.4 mg
Sodium	1199.9 mg
Carbohydrates	36.4 g
Protein	10.9 g

Ingredients

2 C. shredded roast beef
1 C. salsa
1/2 C. roasted red pepper, drained and chopped
1/2 C. Monterey Jack cheese, shredded
1/2 C. cheddar cheese, shredded
1 tsp. cumin

18 inches refrigerated pie crusts

Directions

1. Set your oven to 425 degrees F before doing anything else and grease a baking sheet.
2. In a bowl, add the roast beef, salsa, cheeses, peppers and cumin and mix until well combined.
3. Place each pie crust onto a lightly floured surface and roll each into a 12-inch circle.
4. Place the beef mixture onto 1 crust, mounding into 4 equal sized portions.
5. Cover with the second crust and with a pizza cutter, cut into 4 equal sized wedges.
6. With your fingers, press the edges to seal.
7. In the bottom of the prepared baking sheet, arrange the empanadas.
8. With a knife, make small slits in the top of each empanada.
9. Cook in the oven for about 15 minutes.
10. Enjoy warm.

Empanadas
La Arabia

🥣 Prep Time: 30 mins
🕐 Total Time: 50 mins

Servings per Recipe: 8
Calories	114.6 kcal
Fat	5.6 g
Cholesterol	71.2 mg
Sodium	242.2 mg
Carbohydrates	4.4 g
Protein	11.8 g

Ingredients

Filling
1 lb. lean ground turkey
1 red pepper, diced
4 oz. mushrooms, sliced
1 small onion, diced
2 green onions, sliced
3 garlic cloves, minced
1 tsp. paprika
1 tsp. baharat

1 tsp. cumin
1/2 tsp. salt
3 tsp. curry powder
2 tbsp. tomato paste
1/4 C. water
Pastry
2 (14 oz.) packages goya discos, defrosted
1 egg, beaten

Directions

1. Set your oven to 450 degrees F before doing anything else and grease a baking sheet.
2. In a skillet, add the ground turkey and cook until browned completely.
3. Drain the grease from the turkey.
4. Add the onion, green onion, mushrooms, red pepper and garlic and cook for about 5-6 minutes.
5. Add the tomato paste, spices, salt and water and stir until well combined.
6. Remove from the heat and keep aside to cool.
7. Place each disco onto wax paper piece.
8. Place 1-2 tbsp. of the filling onto one side of each disco.
9. Fold the dough over the filling and press the edges to seal.
10. In the bottom of the prepared baking sheet, arrange the empanadas and coat the top of each with the beaten egg.
11. Cook in the oven for about 10 minutes.
12. Enjoy warm.

GEORGIA
Empanadas

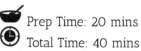 Prep Time: 20 mins

Total Time: 40 mins

Servings per Recipe: 8

Calories	373.8 kcal
Fat	26.0 g
Cholesterol	34.8 mg
Sodium	127.4 mg
Carbohydrates	31.2 g
Protein	5.4 g

Ingredients

12 oz. puff pastry
all-purpose flour, for dusting
3 fresh peaches
2/3 C. sour cream
4 tbsp. brown sugar
4-5 tbsp. pecans (toasted and finely
chopped)

1 egg, beaten
superfine sugar, for sprinkling

Directions

1. Set your oven to 400 degrees F before doing anything else and grease a baking sheet.
2. Place the pastry onto a lightly floured surface and roll into an even thickness.
3. Cut 8 (6-inch) circles from the dough.
4. In a heatproof bowl, place the peaches and enough boiling water to cover.
5. Keep aside for about 4-5 seconds.
6. Drain the peaches and remove the skins.
7. Cut each peach in half and remove the pits.
8. Cut the flesh into slices.
9. Place a spoonful of sour cream on one half of each dough circle and top with peach slices evenly, followed by a little brown sugar and nuts.
10. Coat the edges with the beaten egg.
11. Fold the dough over the filling and press the edges to seal.
12. With a fork, prick the top of each empanada.
13. In the bottom of the prepared baking sheet, arrange the empanadas.
14. Coat each empanada with the beaten egg and sprinkle with the superfine sugar.
15. Cook in the oven for about 20 minutes.
16. Enjoy warm.

Sunday
Morning Empanadas

🥣 Prep Time: 1 hr 10 mins
🕐 Total Time: 1 hr 40 mins

Servings per Recipe: 12
Calories	128.8 kcal
Fat	8.3 g
Cholesterol	70.5 mg
Sodium	219.3 mg
Carbohydrates	9.2 g
Protein	4.8 g

Ingredients

1/2 C. all-purpose flour
1/2 C. whole wheat flour
1/2 C. soy flour
1/3 C. vegetable shortening
6 tbsp. ice water
1 tbsp. apple cider vinegar
4 eggs
1/2 C. Baby Spinach
2 tsp. curry powder
2 tsp. paprika

1 tsp. salt

Directions

1. Set your oven to 400 degrees F before doing anything else and grease a baking sheet.
2. For the dough: in a bowl, add the all-purpose flour, vinegar and water and mix until well combined.
3. Add the remaining ingredients and with a pastry cutter, mix until a dough forms.
4. Make 2 disks from the dough.
5. With a plastic wrap, cover the dough and refrigerate for about 1 hour.
6. For the filling: in a lightly greased pan, add the eggs and cook until scrambled.
7. Stir in the spices and spinach and cook until just wilted.
8. Place the dough onto a lightly floured surface and roll into an even thickness.
9. Now, cut the dough into circles.
10. Place 1-2 tbsp. of onto the center of each dough circle.
11. Fold the dough over the filling and press the edges to seal.
12. In the bottom of the prepared baking sheet, arrange the empanadas.

13. Cook in the oven for about 15 minutes.
14. Enjoy warm.

Carmen's
Empanadas

Prep Time: 2 hrs

Total Time: 2 hr 30 mins

Servings per Recipe: 8

Calories	949.7 kcal
Fat	76.3 g
Cholesterol	156.4 mg
Sodium	481.1 mg
Carbohydrates	30.1 g
Protein	35.5 g

Ingredients

Beef
1 C. chopped onion
3 garlic cloves, crushed
2 lb. beef stew meat, trimmed and cut into
1-inch pieces
1 C. beef broth
1 tsp. sugar
1/2 tsp. crushed red pepper flakes
1 unpeeled orange wedge, large
Filling

2 C. vertically sliced onions
1 C. sliced green bell pepper
1 C. chopped seeded tomatoes
1/4 tsp. crushed red pepper flakes
1/4 tsp. salt
3 C. beef, carnita filling
2 refrigerated pie crusts

Directions

1. For the beef carnita: place a greased Dutch oven over medium-high heat until heated through.
2. Add the onion and stir fry for about 4 minutes.
3. Add the beef and garlic and stir fry for about 5 minutes.
4. Add the sugar, salt, pepper and water and stir to combine.
5. Gently, push the orange section into the beef mixture and cook until boiling.
6. Set the heat to low and cook for about 1 1/2 hours.
7. Remove the orange section and cook, uncovered for about 8 minutes, mixing frequently.
8. For the filling: place a greased nonstick skillet over medium-high heat until heated through.
9. Add the bell pepper and onion and stir fry for about 4-5 minutes.
10. Stir in the tomato, 1/4 tsp. of the salt and red pepper and stir fry for about 2 minutes.
11. Stir in the beef carnitas and cook for about 2 minutes, mixing frequently.

12. Remove from the heat and keep aside to cool.
13. Set your oven to 400 degrees F and grease a baking sheet.
14. Place each pie dough onto a lightly floured surface and roll each piece into a 11-inch circle.
15. In the bottom of the prepared baking sheet, arrange 1 dough circle.
16. Place the filling onto the dough circle, leaving about 1-inch edge.
17. Cover with the remaining dough and press the edges to seal.
18. With a knife, cut slits on the top of dough.
19. Cook in the oven for about 30 minutes.
20. Cut into 8 wedges and enjoy warm.

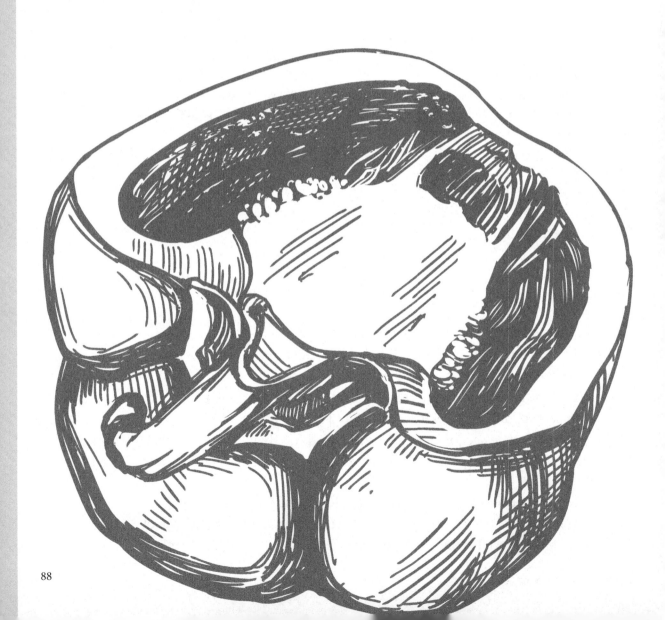

Cheddar
Crème Empanadas

🥣 Prep Time: 40 mins
🕐 Total Time: 1 hr 55 mins

Servings per Recipe: 6	
Calories	673.6
Fat	40.1 g
Cholesterol	67.3 mg
Sodium	720.3 mg
Carbohydrates	49.4 g
Protein	29.0 g

Ingredients

1 lb. short crust pastry
2 tbsp. olive oil
2 lb. onions, sliced
2 garlic cloves, crushed
2 tbsp. sun-dried tomato paste
14 oz. tuna in vegetable oil, drained
3 tbsp. crème fraiche

2 oz. sharp cheddar cheese, finely grated
salt & freshly ground black pepper
20 basil leaves
1 egg, beaten

Directions

1. Set your oven to 400 degrees F before doing anything else and grease a baking sheet.
2. Place half of the pastry onto a floured surface and roll into a 12x8-inch rectangle.
3. In the bottom of the prepared baking sheet, arrange the dough rectangle and place in the fridge for about 10 minutes.
4. With a fork, prick the pastry rectangle and cook in the oven for about 15 minutes. Bake
5. Remove from the oven and keep aside to cool.
6. In a heavy-based skillet, the olive oil and cook until heated.
7. Add the onion and cook for about 20 minutes, stirring occasionally.
8. Increase the heat to medium.
9. Add the garlic and stir fry until the onions become golden brown.
10. Transfer the onion into a bowl and keep aside to cool.
11. In another bowl, add the tuna, sun-dried tomato paste, Cheddar, creme fraiche, salt and ground pepper and mix until well combined.
12. Place the tuna mixture onto the cooled pastry base evenly, leaving 1/2-inch border and top with the cooked onions and basil leaves.
13. Coat the edge with the beaten egg.

14. Place the remaining pastry onto a floured surface and roll into a large rectangle.

15. Place the pastry over the tuna filling and press the edges to seal.

16. Coat the top with the beaten egg.

17. Cook in the oven for about 35-40 minutes.

18. Enjoy warm.

19. Cook in the oven for about 35-40 minutes.

20. Enjoy warm.

Summer
Empanadas

🍲 Prep Time: 1 hr

🕐 Total Time: 1 hr 25 mins

Servings per Recipe: 6

Calories	681.1 kcal
Fat	31.9 g
Cholesterol	35.2 mg
Sodium	20.3 mg
Carbohydrates	89.7 g
Protein	11.0 g

Ingredients

3 1/2 C. flour
3/4 C. vegetable shortening
salt and pepper
2 tbsp. extra virgin olive oil
3 lb. Spanish onions, thinly sliced
1/2 C. coarsely chopped dates
1 tsp. balsamic vinegar

1 large egg
2 oz. crumbled tart cheese (blue, feta, goat)

Directions

1. In a food processor, add the flour, 1 tsp. of the salt and shortening and pulse until a sand like mixture forms.
2. While the motor is running, slowly add 1 C. of the cold water and pulse until a dough ball is formed.
3. Divide the dough into 2 equal sized circles.
4. With a plastic wrap, cover the dough circles and place in the fridge for about 30 minutes.
5. In a skillet, add the oil and 1/2 C. of the water over high heat until heated.
6. Add the onions and cook for about 10 minutes.
7. Set the heat to low and cook for about 30 minutes, mixing occasionally.
8. Remove from the heat and stir in the dates, vinegar, salt and pepper.
9. Keep aside to cool.
10. Set your oven to 400 degrees F and line 2 baking sheets with the parchment paper.
11. Place the dough rounds onto a lightly floured surface and cut each into 6 equal sized circles.
12. Now, roll each piece into a thin circle.
13. In a bowl, add the egg and 1 tsp. of the water and beat well.

14. Place the onion mixture onto each dough circle and top each with 1 tsp. of the cheese.
15. Coat the edges with the egg wash.
16. Fold the dough over the filling and press the edges to seal.
17. In the bottom of the prepared baking sheets, arrange the empanadas.
18. Cook in the oven for about 20-25 minutes.
19. Enjoy warm.

Picnic
Empanadas

Prep Time: 0 mins
Total Time: 30 mins

Servings per Recipe: 1
Calories	189.6 kcal
Fat	10.0 g
Cholesterol	8.4 mg
Sodium	422.9 mg
Carbohydrates	21.2 g
Protein	3.5 g

Ingredients

5 C. all-purpose flour
1 C. margarine
1 tbsp. baking powder
1 C. soy milk
1 tbsp. salt
1 egg
1 1/2 lb. ground meat
2 large white onions, diced

1/4 C. oil
1 dash salt
1 dash cumin
1 dash cayenne pepper
1 tbsp. flour
5 eggs, hardboiled
3/4 C. golden raisin
30 black olives

Directions

1. For the dough: in a bowl, add the flour and baking powder and mix well.
2. With a pastry blender, cut in the margarine until a crumbly mixture is formed.
3. In a pan, add the soy milk and 1 tbsp. of the salt and cook until heated through.
4. Add the hot milk mixture into the flour mixture and mix until well combined.
5. With a tea towel, cover the dough and keep aside for about 30 minutes.
6. For the filling: in a pan, add the oil and cook until heated through.
7. Add the ground meat, onion, raisins and spices and stir to combine.
8. St the heat to low and cook for about 15 minute.
9. Remove from the heat and stir in 1 tbsp. of the flour.
10. Keep aside to cool.
11. Set your oven to 350 degrees F before doing anything else and grease a baking sheet.
12. Place the dough onto a floured surface and roll into an even thickness.
13. Now, cut the dough into large circles.
14. Place about 1 heaping tbsp. of the meat mixture onto each circle, followed by 1 egg slice, and 1 black olive.

15. With wet fingers, moisten the edges of each circle.

16. Fold the dough over the filling and press the edges to seal.

17. In the bottom of the prepared baking sheet, arrange the empanadas.

18. Cook in the oven for about 30 - 35 minutes.

19. Enjoy warm.

Curried
Madrasala Empanadas

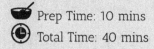 Prep Time: 10 mins
Total Time: 40 mins

Servings per Recipe: 4
Calories	76.1 kcal
Fat	1.8 g
Cholesterol	52.8 mg
Sodium	72.1 mg
Carbohydrates	11.4 g
Protein	5.2 g

Ingredients

8 empanada wrappers
1 (10 oz.) boxes frozen chopped spinach
1/4 vidalia onion, chopped
1 small baking potato, diced
2 tbsp. chopped garlic
curry seasoning
garam masala seasoning

shredded mozzarella cheese
1 egg, beaten

Directions

1. In a greased skillet, add the potato and onion and cook until potato is crisp tender.
2. Add the spinach, garlic and 1/2 tsp. of the curry seasoning and 1/2 tsp. of the garam masala seasoning and cook until desired doneness of the potatoes.
3. Remove from the heat and keep aside for about 10-15 minutes.
4. Set your oven to 400 degrees F and grease a baking sheet.
5. Place about 2 tbsp. of the spinach mixture onto each empanada wrapper top with the cheese.
6. Fold the dough over the filling and press the edges to seal.
7. In the bottom of the prepared baking sheet, arrange the empanadas and coat the top of each with the beaten egg.
8. Cook in the oven for about 18 minutes.
9. Enjoy warm.

EMPANADAS
Guzman

Prep Time: 25 mins
Total Time: 40 mins

Servings per Recipe: 1
Calories   65.4 kcal
Fat   2.1 g
Cholesterol   11.9 mg
Sodium   112.1 mg
Carbohydrates   8.8 g
Protein   2.7 g

Ingredients

1/2 lb. ground beef
1/3 C. chopped green pepper
3 tbsp. dry onion soup mix
1/4 C. chopped black olives
1/4 C. raisins
1/4 C. ketchup
1/8 tsp. crushed red pepper flakes

2 (8 oz.) packages refrigerated crescent dinner rolls

Directions

1. Set your oven to 375 degrees F before doing anything else.
2. In a skillet, add the ground beef and green pepper and cook until meat is browned.
3. Stir in the olives, instant onion soup, ketchup, raisins and red pepper flakes and remove from the heat.
4. Separate the crescent dough as suggested on the package.
5. Divide the dough in half and roll each in a triangle.
6. Place spoonful of the beef mixture onto the center of each triangle.
7. Fold the dough over the filling and press the edges to seal.
8. In the bottom of an ungreased baking sheet, arrange the empanadas.
9. Cook in the oven for about 15 minutes.
10. Enjoy warm.

Empanada
Seduction

Prep Time: 1 mins
Total Time: 10 mins

Servings per Recipe: 6

Calories	300.1 kcal
Fat	5.4 g
Cholesterol	0.0 mg
Sodium	454.6 mg
Carbohydrates	56.2 g
Protein	5.9 g

Ingredients

1 (10 inch) flour tortillas
2 tbsp. fat free cream cheese
1 1/2 tbsp. raspberry preserves
cinnamon
Hershey's dark chocolate syrup
powdered sugar

Directions

1. In a bowl, add the preserves and cream cheese and mix until well combined.
2. Coat one side of each tortilla with the cooking spray and sprinkle with the cinnamon.
3. Place a greased nonstick skillet over medium heat and cook until heated through.
4. Place 1 tortilla, at a time, cinnamon side down and cook until just softened.
5. Place the cream cheese mixture onto the tortilla and roll it.
6. Spray the outsides with the cooking spray cook until golden brown, flipping frequently.
7. Enjoy warm with a drizzling of the chocolate syrup.

HOT
Carolina Empanadas

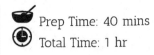

Prep Time: 40 mins
Total Time: 1 hr

Servings per Recipe: 12
Calories	513.3 kcal
Fat	35.7 g
Cholesterol	93.1 mg
Sodium	1125.7 mg
Carbohydrates	22.2 g
Protein	25.6 g

Ingredients

Empanadas
3 C. chopped cooked chicken
1 (8 oz.) packages shredded Colby-
Monterey Jack cheese
4 oz. cream cheese, softened
1 chopped red bell pepper
1 jalapeño, seeded and chopped
1 tbsp. ground cumin
1 1/2 tsp. salt

1/2 tsp. ground black pepper
1 (15 oz.) packages refrigerated pie crusts
water
Cheese Dip
1 lb. cheddar cheese
1 (16 oz.) cans diced tomatoes, drained
1 (4 oz.) cans diced green chilies
2 tsp. hot sauce

Directions

1. In a bowl, add the chicken, cream cheese, cheese blend, jalapeno, red pepper, cumin, salt, and pepper and mix until well combined.
2. Place each pie crust onto a lightly floured surface and roll into 15-inch circle.
3. With a 3-inch cookie cutter, cut circles from the dough.
4. Place 1 heaping tsp. of the chicken mixture in the center of each dough circle.
5. With wet fingers, moisten the edges of each circle.
6. Fold the dough over the filling and press the edges to seal.
7. In a deep skillet, add the oil and cook until its temperature reaches to 350 degrees F.
8. Add the empanadas in batches and cook for about 3-5 minutes
9. With a slotted spoon, transfer the empanadas onto a paper towels-lined plate to drain.
10. Meanwhile, for the dip: in a pan, add the Cheddar over medium-low heat and cook until melted.
11. Add the chiles, tomatoes and hot sauce and cook until well combined, mixing continuously.
12. Enjoy warm empanadas alongside the dip.

Chicago
Deep Dish Empanadas

🥣 Prep Time: 30 mins
🕐 Total Time: 40 mins

Servings per Recipe: 9
Calories   309.1 kcal
Fat   11.9 g
Cholesterol   43.1 mg
Sodium   656.7 mg
Carbohydrates   37.7 g
Protein   11.8 g

Ingredients

Dough
3 C. flour
1 tsp. salt
1/2 C. cold water
1 egg
1 egg white
1 tsp. vinegar

3 tbsp. shortening
Filling
1 (15 oz.) cans pizza sauce
2 C. shredded mozzarella cheese
1 1/2 C. pepperoni
oil

Directions

1. In a bowl, add the egg, egg white, water and vinegar and beat until well combined.
2. In another bowl, add the flour and salt and mix well.
3. With a pastry blender, cut in the shortening until a crumbly mixture forms.
4. With your hands, make a well in the center of the flour mixture.
5. In the well, add the egg mixture and with a fork, mix until a stiff dough forms.
6. Place the dough onto a lightly floured surface and with your hands, knead until a smooth dough forms.
7. With a plastic wrap, cover the dough and place in the fridge for about 2-24 hours.
8. Place the dough onto a floured surface and roll into 1/8-inch thickness.
9. With a 6-inch round biscuit cutter, cut the dough into circles.
10. Place the pizza sauces onto each dough circle evenly, leaving a little border and top each with the cheese, followed by the pepperoni pieces.
11. With wet fingers, moisten the edges of each circle.
12. Fold the dough over the filling and press the edges to seal.
13. In a deep skillet, add the oil and cook until its temperature reaches to 360 degrees F.
14. Add the empanadas in batches and cook until golden brown.
15. With a slotted spoon, transfer the empanadas onto a paper towels-lined plate to drain.
16. Enjoy warm.

DESSERT
Empanadas 101

 Prep Time: 1 hr 10 mins

Total Time: 2 hrs 40 mins

Servings per Recipe: 1
Calories	157.2 kcal
Fat	8.2 g
Cholesterol	22.7 mg
Sodium	140.6 mg
Carbohydrates	20.8 g
Protein	2.9 g

Ingredients

4 large ripe bananas
2 tbsp. sugar
1 tsp. cinnamon
4 oz. semisweet chocolate, broken in chunks
confectioners' sugar, for dusting
Dough
1 1/2 C. all-purpose flour

1 C. masa harina
1 tsp. baking powder
1 tsp. salt
1/2 C. unsalted butter, melted and cooled
1 large egg, beaten with 1 tbsp. water, for egg wash
butter, for greasing the pans

Directions

1. For the dough: in a bowl, add the masa harina, flour, baking powder and salt and mix well.
2. Now, sift the flour mixture into a second bowl.
3. Add the melted butter and mix well.
4. Slowly, add 1/2-3/4 C. of the water and with your hands, mix until a dough ball forms.
5. With a plastic wrap, cover the dough ball and refrigerate for about 30 minutes.
6. In a bowl, add the bananas, sugar and cinnamon and with a fork, mash until just creamy.
7. Place the dough onto a lightly floured surface and cut into 2 equal sized pieces.
8. Roll each dough piece into 1/8-inch thickness.
9. With a 4-inch biscuit cutter, cut 10 circles from the dough.
10. Place 2 tbsp. of the banana mixture onto the center of each dough circle, leaving about 1/2-inch edge and slightly, press 1 chocolate piece on top.
11. Coat the edges with the egg wash.
12. Fold the dough over the filling and press the edges to seal.
13. In a tray, arrange the empanadas and refrigerate for about 30 minutes.
14. Set your oven to 375 degrees F before doing anything else and grease a baking sheet.

Dessert Empanadas 101

15. Coat the top of each empanada with the egg wash and with a fork, prick each one.
16. Cook in the oven for about 30 minutes.
17. Enjoy warm.

SOUTHWEST
King Shrimp Empanadas

Prep Time: 25 mins
Total Time: 55 mins

Servings per Recipe: 12

Calories	169.6 kcal
Fat	4.2 g
Cholesterol	73.3 mg
Sodium	301.7 mg
Carbohydrates	22.6 g
Protein	9.5 g

Ingredients

2 1/2 C. plain flour
1/2 C. sour cream
1 egg
2 tbsp. water, chilled
1/4 tsp. sea salt
1/2 tsp. white pepper
1 tbsp. olive oil
1 small red onion, small, finely chopped
2 garlic cloves, finely chopped

1 tsp. ground cumin
500 g green prawns, peeled & finely chopped
2 tomatoes, diced
1 small red chili pepper, small- finely chopped
2 tbsp. milk
coriander

Directions

1. In a blender, add the egg, sour cream, water, salt and pepper and pulse until well combined.
2. Place the dough onto a lightly floured surface and with your hands, pat into a circle.
3. With a plastic wrap, cover the dough and place in the fridge for about 20-25 minutes.
4. For the filling: in a pan, add the oil over medium heat and cook until heated through.
5. Add the onion and stir fry for about 3-4 minutes.
6. Add the prawn, tomato, garlic, chili, cumin and coriander and cook for about 5-6 minutes, mixing occasionally.
7. Remove from the heat and keep aside to cool.
8. Set your oven to 350 degrees F and line a baking sheet with the parchment paper.
9. Arrange the dough circle between 2 parchment papers and roll into 1/4-inch thickness.
10. With a 4 3/4-inch round cutter, cut the circles from the dough.
11. Place a tbsp. of the filling onto the center of each dough circle.
12. Fold the dough over the filling and press the edges to seal.

13. In the bottom of the prepared baking sheet, arrange the empanadas. and coat each with the milk.
14. Cook in the oven for about 15-20 minutes.
15. Enjoy warm.

CUBAN
Empanadas

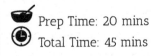

Prep Time: 20 mins
Total Time: 45 mins

Servings per Recipe: 4
Calories	556.5 kcal
Fat	44.4 g
Cholesterol	170.7 mg
Sodium	379.1 mg
Carbohydrates	21.2 g
Protein	16.9 g

Ingredients

1 lb. cubed steak
1/2 lb. soda cracker
5 eggs
3 tbsp. adobo seasoning
6 garlic cloves
1/2 C. apple cider vinegar
1 C. oil

Directions

1. With a mortar and pestle, crush the garlic cloves.
2. Add the adobo seasoning and mix well.
3. In a bowl, add the eggs and beat well.
4. In another bowl, add the vinegar and oil and beat well.
5. Add the garlic paste and mix well.
6. Coat the meat with the oil mixture generously, followed by the beaten eggs and crushed crackers.
7. In a deep skillet, add the oil over medium heat and cook until heated through.
8. Add the meat and cook for about 15 minutes.
9. Now, set the heat to high and cook until golden brown.

Queso
Blanco and Beans Empanadas

Prep Time: 45 mins
Total Time: 1 hr 30 mins

Servings per Recipe: 6

Calories	886.1 kcal
Fat	87.0 g
Cholesterol	52.8 mg
Sodium	595.7 mg
Carbohydrates	23.0 g
Protein	6.3 g

Ingredients

Filling
1 tbsp. olive oil
1/4 C. finely diced onion
3/4 tsp. minced garlic
1/4 tsp. cumin
1/4 tsp. dried Mexican oregano, crumbled
1 1/2 C. cooked black beans
1 tsp. salt
1/4 tsp. pepper
3 tbsp. water
1/4 C. crumbled queso blanco

Dough
3/4 C. flour
1/2 C. masa harina
1 1/2 tsp. baking powder
3/4 tsp. salt
1 tbsp. canola oil
2 large eggs
2 tbsp. water
egg wash
3 C. oil
kosher salt, as needed for garnish

Directions

1. For the filling: in a skillet, add the oil
2. Over medium-high heat and cook until heated through.
3. Add the onion and garlic and stir fry for about 4-5 minutes.
4. Stir in the oregano and cumin and stir fry for about 30 seconds.
5. Stir in the beans, salt and pepper and remove from the heat.
6. Keep aside to cool slightly.
7. In a food processor, add the beans and a little water and pulse until a smooth puree is formed.
8. Transfer the pureed beans into a bowl with the cheese and mix well.
9. For the dough: in a bowl, add the masa harina, flour, baking powder and salt and mix well.
10. Add the oil and with a wooden spoon., mix until well combined.

11. In another bowl, add the water and eggs and beat until well combined.
12. Slowly, add the egg mixture into the flour mixture and mix until well combined.
13. Place the dough onto a lightly floured surface and with your hands, knead for about 3 minutes.
14. Roll the dough into 1/16-inch thickness.
15. With a 3-inch cookie cutter, cut circles from the dough.
16. In a bowl, add 1 egg and 1 tbsp. of the water and beat well.
17. Place about 2 1/2 tsp. of the filling in the center of each dough circle.
18. Coat the edges of each dough circle with the egg wash.
19. Fold the dough over the filling and press the edges to seal.
20. In a deep skillet, add the oil and cook until its temperature reaches to 350 degrees F.
21. Add the empanadas in batches and cook for about 3-4 minutes.
22. With a slotted spoon, transfer the empanadas onto a paper towels-lined plate to drain.
23. Enjoy warm.

Alaskan
Empanadas

🥣 Prep Time: 30 mins
🕐 Total Time: 50 mins

Servings per Recipe: 16
Calories   165.2 kcal
Fat   10.7 g
Cholesterol   5.7 mg
Sodium   264.1 mg
Carbohydrates   13.5 g
Protein   3.4 g

Ingredients

Empanadas
1 (15 oz.) boxes Pillsbury refrigerated pie crusts
6 oz. smoked salmon, flaked
1 (5 1/4 oz.) packages boursin spreadable cheese with garlic and herbs
Dip

1/2 C. sour cream
1 tbsp. chopped chives, if desired
paprika, for sprinkling

Directions

1. Set your oven to 425 degrees F before doing anything else and line a baking sheet with the parchment paper.
2. Arrange the pie crusts onto a smooth surface.
3. Cut each crust into 4 wedges.
4. In a bowl, add the cheese and salmon and mix well.
5. Place about 2 tbsp. of the salmon mixture onto half of each crust wedge, leaving 1/4-inch border.
6. With wet fingers, moisten the edges of each wedge.
7. Fold the dough over the filling to form the triangles and press the edges to seal.
8. In the bottom of the prepared baking sheet, arrange the empanadas.
9. Cook in the oven for about 12-17 minutes.
10. Enjoy warm.
11. Remove from the oven and place the baking sheets onto a wire rack for about 10 minutes.
12. For the dip: in a bowl, add the sour cream, chives and paprika and gently, stir to combine.
13. Cut each empanada in half and enjoy alongside the dip.

GROUND
Beef Empanadas

 Prep Time: 40 mins
🕐 Total Time: 58 mins

Servings per Recipe: 9
Calories   358.0 kcal
Fat   20.5 g
Cholesterol   59.3 mg
Sodium   129.9 mg
Carbohydrates   33.1 g
Protein   9.7 g

Ingredients

6 oz. lean ground beef
1/3 C. finely chopped onion
1 minced garlic clove
1/2 tsp. ground cumin
1/8 tsp. ground red pepper
1/2 C. chopped pimento stuffed olive
1/4 C. tomato sauce

3 C. all-purpose flour
1/4 tsp. salt
3/4 C. shortening
1 beaten egg
1/2 C. water
1 egg
1 tbsp. water

Directions

1. For the filling: in a skillet, add the beef, onion and garlic and cook until meat is browned.
2. Drain the grease from the beef mixture.
3. Stir in the red pepper and cumin and cook for about 1 minute.
4. Stir in the tomato sauce and olives and remove from the heat.
5. Keep aside to cool.
6. Set your oven to 425 degrees F.
7. For the dough: in a bowl, add the flour and salt and mix well.
8. With a pastry blender, cut in the shortening until a cornmeal like mixture forms.
9. Add the beaten egg and 1/2 C. of the water and mix until blended nicely.
10. Place the dough onto a lightly floured surface and with your hands, knead for about 10-12 times.
11. Cut the dough into 2 equal sized pieces and roll each into 1/8-inch thickness.
12. With a 3-inch cookie cutter, cut circles from each dough piece.
13. Place about 1 rounded tsp. of the filling onto the center of each circle.
14. With wet fingers, moisten the edges of each circle.
15. Fold the dough over the filling and press the edges to seal.

16. In a bowl, add the egg and water and beat well.
17. In the bottom of an ungreased baking sheet, arrange the empanadas and coat each with the egg wash.
18. Cook in the oven for about 15-18 minutes.
19. Enjoy warm.

CHILI
Empanadas

Prep Time: 20 mins
Total Time: 45 mins

Servings per Recipe: 4
Calories	351.6 kcal
Fat	15.0 g
Cholesterol	63.3 mg
Sodium	558.3 mg
Carbohydrates	28.9 g
Protein	23.3 g

Ingredients

cooking spray
3 1/2 C. diced baking potatoes
1 C. chopped onion
1 1/4 lb. ground sirloin
1 1/2 tsp. dried oregano
1 1/2 tsp. chili powder
1 tsp. ground cumin
1/2 tsp. salt
1 dash black pepper
2 large garlic cloves, minced

1/3 C. all-purpose flour
1/2 C. beer
1 (10 1/2 oz.) cans beef consomme
1 (14 1/2 oz.) cans diced tomatoes with green pepper and onion, drained
2 tbsp. chopped pitted green olives
1 tbsp. cider vinegar
1 (10 5/8 oz.) boxes refrigerated garlic bread sticks

Directions

1. Set your oven to 350 degrees F before doing anything else and grease a baking sheet.
2. Set your oven to 350 degrees F before doing anything else and grease an 11x7-inch baking dish.
3. For the filling: Place a greased heavy-bottomed pan over medium heat until heated through.
4. Add the onion and potato and cook, covered for about 7 minutes, mixing often.
5. Add the beef, garlic, oregano, chili powder, cumin, salt and black pepper and cook, uncovered for about 7-8 minutes, breaking up the meat.
6. Stir in the flour and cook for about 1 minute.
7. Slowly, add the beer, tomatoes and consommé and cook until boiling.
8. Remove from the heat and stir in the vinegar and olives.
9. In the bottom of the prepared baking dish, place the beef mixture evenly.
10. Unroll both dough portions and then, roll together into a 12x10-inch rectangle.

11. Arrange the dough on top of beef mixture and press the edges.
12. With a knife, cut 5 slits in top of crust.
13. Coat the top of the crust with 1 tbsp. of the garlic spread.
14. Cook in the oven for about 25 minutes.
15. Enjoy warm.

ARIZONA
Monterey Empanadas

 Prep Time: 1 hr

Total Time: 1 hr 15 mins

Servings per Recipe: 1
Calories	104.5 kcal
Fat	6.9 g
Cholesterol	11.1 mg
Sodium	67.9 mg
Carbohydrates	7.1 g
Protein	3.4 g

Ingredients

2 1/2 C. chopped cooked chicken
1/2 C. Monterey Jack pepper cheese
1/2 C. chunky salsa
2 tbsp. chopped fresh cilantro
1 tsp. ground cumin
2 tbsp. sour cream
1 tbsp. finely chopped jalapeño pepper

3 sheets frozen puff pastry, thawed for 30 minutes
1 large egg
1 tbsp. water

Directions

1. Set your oven to 400 degrees F before doing anything else and grease a baking sheet.
2. In a bowl, add the chicken, sour cream, cheese, salsa, jalapeño, cilantro and cumin and mix until well combined.
3. Place each puff pastry sheet onto a lightly floured surface and roll into a 13-inch square.
4. With a 3-inch round cutter, cut pastry into 16 equal sized circles.
5. Place 1 tsp. of the chicken mixture onto the center of each circle.
6. With wet fingers, moisten the edges of each circle.
7. Fold the dough over the filling and press the edges to seal.
8. In a small bowl, add the egg and water and beat well.
9. In the bottom of the prepared baking sheet, arrange the empanadas.
10. Coat each empanada with the egg wash.
11. Cook in the oven for about 12-15 minutes.
12. Enjoy warm

Chicken
Biscuit Empanadas

Prep Time: 20 mins
Total Time: 30 mins

Servings per Recipe: 1

Calories	106.1 kcal
Fat	5.5 g
Cholesterol	27.7 mg
Sodium	125.8 mg
Carbohydrates	7.5 g
Protein	6.2 g

Ingredients

1 (9 3/4 oz.) cans chicken breasts, drained,
or cans tuna
1/4 tsp. black pepper
1/2 C. cheddar cheese, shredded
3 oz. cream cheese
1 (8 oz.) cans biscuits

Directions

1. Set your oven to 375 degrees F before doing anything else and grease a baking sheet.
2. In a bowl, add the chicken and with a fork shred the meat.
3. Add the cream cheese, cheddar and pepper and mix until well combined.
4. With your hands, flatten each biscuit.
5. Place about 1 tbsp. of the chicken mixture onto the center of each biscuit.
6. Fold the dough over the filling and press the edges to seal.
7. In the bottom of the prepared baking sheet, arrange the empanadas and spray with the cooking spray.
8. Cook in the oven for about 8-10 minutes, rotating the baking sheet once half way through.
9. Enjoy warm

HOW
to Make Dulce de Leche

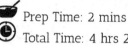 Prep Time: 2 mins
Total Time: 4 hrs 2 mins

Servings per Recipe: 1
Calories	171.6 kcal
Fat	4.6 g
Cholesterol	18.1 mg
Sodium	67.9 mg
Carbohydrates	29.0 g
Protein	4.2 g

Ingredients

1 can sweetened condensed milk

Directions

1. Use a sharp knife of a bottle opener to pierce the top of the milk can.
2. Remove the paper from the can and discard it.
3. Place a large saucepan over medium heat. Place in it the milk can and pour it in the saucepan enough water to cover 1 inch of the can.
4. Wrap a small piece of oil on top of the can and let it cook for 4 h over low medium heat.
5. Once the time is up, discard the foil and open the milk can. Serve your dulce de leche with some cut up fruits, crackers.
6. Enjoy.

Made in the USA
Middletown, DE
20 November 2021

52999110R00064